I0616537

SPOKEN TELUGU
FOR ABSOLUTE BEGINNERS

SANJAY D

Expert in Language Training

Book Title: Spoken Telugu for Absolute Beginners

Book Author: Sanjay D

Published by Sanjay D

Printed and bound by Amazon

This edition published in: 2019

ISBN Print: 978-93-5361-896-4

Copyright © Sanjay D 2019

Sanjay D asserts the moral right to be identified as the author of this work.

This book is a work of fiction and any resemblance to actual persons, living or dead, events and locales is purely coincidental.

All rights reserved. No part of this publication may be reproduced, stored in or introduced into a retrieval system, or transmitted, in any form, or by any means (electrical, mechanical, photocopying, recording or otherwise) without the prior written permission of the author or publisher. Any person who does any unauthorized act in relation to this publication may be liable to criminal prosecution and civil claims for damages.

Acknowledgement and Dedications

First and foremost, I would like to thank my mom Meenakshi and my wife Jacqueline for standing beside me throughout my career and helping me to write this book. They have been my inspiration and motivation for continuing to improve my knowledge and write this book. They are my rock, and I dedicate this book to them. I also dedicate this book to all Telugu learners in the world who wants to connect with their loved ones, who wants to enjoy the beauty of the language and more that's being offered by the Beautiful and elegant Telugu.

Special thanks to

Aswani Kopparapu, a Telugu tutor and language trainer. She loves Telugu language more than anybody I know of and is a kind hearted person. She has been a huge support for me and helped me in writing this book. Also, I would like to thank Maheshwaran A. R. for illustrating the book cover and helping me with the audio for this book.

Table of Contents

INTRODUCTION

About the Author:

Sanjay D was born and raised in the southern part of India. He has always been fascinated with south Indian languages and loved them with all his heart. He started teaching south Indian languages to several foreigners, and through that, he came to understand the difficulty foreigners have in learning them. So, he prepared an organized and systematic course to help them learn and speak the language with ease and better pronunciation. This book is the ultimate result of years of experience in teaching South Indian languages to Indians and foreigners.

About Telugu:

Telugu is a Dravidian language spoken by more than 81 million people worldwide. Telugu is spoken predominantly in India. In India, Telugu is the mother tongue of people in the state of Andhra Pradesh and Telangana. Over many years, Telugu speakers have migrated to other countries like Singapore, Malaysia, USA, Canada, UK, Germany, etc. Telugu is one of the longest-surviving classical languages in the world. It is also stated as 15th in the Ethnologue list of most-spoken languages worldwide. Prakrit Inscriptions with some Telugu words dating back to between 400 BCE and 100 BCE have been discovered in Bhattiprolu in the Guntur district of Andhra Pradesh. The variety and quality of classical Telugu literature have led to its being described as "one of the great classical traditions and literature of the world." Telugu has a very rich culture and a visit to the state of Andhra Pradesh and Telangana will provide you with the opportunity to experience its beauty and the language.

Andhra Pradesh and Telangana are also known for their world-famous food culture; if you visit these states, then you must definitely try their pesarattu (It's a crepe prepared with green gram), Hyderabadi biriyani (It's a dish made with rice and masala), ulavucharu dishes (many dishes made of horse gram) and many more. There is a huge list of dishes that one can try; but, since this is a language book, I should stop here.

IMPORTANT: MUST READ

About This Book:

1) This book is designed in such a way that you do not require any prior knowledge before learning spoken Telugu through this book. This book is meant for beginners, and those who are looking to review, improve their Telugu fluency and understand the language better.

2) Telugu Script:

The best way to learn any language pronunciations independently is to learn the alphabets of that language; but the Telugu language scripts are very broad and detailed with minute changes in the script for various pronunciations, which are also difficult to recognize. This makes the Telugu script very unique, beautiful, and at the same time challenging to learn.

Taking the above points into consideration, I have avoided the Telugu script in this book, so that the readers can directly dive into learning the Telugu Grammar, Telugu sentences and practicing their pronunciation. This will save lots of time and makes it easier to learn the language as well. The pronunciations of the Telugu scripts are provided in the form of simple English Transliteration; I didn't use the IPA pronunciations that are usually used in other books because IPA pronunciation for Telugu is very broad, there are multiple sounds. Hence, everything has to be explained in detail and understood by you clearly before you start to learn Telugu grammar, vocabularies, and sentences. So, I have ignored the IPA pronunciation altogether.

Now the question in your mind will be "Then, how are we supposed to learn and speak in Telugu with proper pronunciation" and the answer would be "while you are learning Telugu from this book, you should focus your attention on the Telugu Transliteration and the mp3 audio provided along with the book". Yes, for every Telugu transliteration, an audio is being provided so that you can listen to the sound and mimic the pronunciation, and the Transliteration will help you as well.

This is a simple trick I formulated after years of teaching this language to foreigners and Indians. Let's say you hire a teacher to teach you a foreign language, e.g., Telugu, Hindi, Chinese, etc. and you don't want to spend time on learning the Alphabets of that language for whatsoever reason. Then the teacher will teach you the vocabularies or the sentences by pronouncing them for you, and you have to repeat them, while the teacher will correct you, and if necessary, the teacher will provide you with the transliteration of the vocabulary or sentence in English. I have employed the same principle here; instead of the teacher pronouncing the vocabularies to you, you will listen to my audio where I will pronounce the vocabulary or sentence for you. Whenever you feel that you are not pronouncing the vocabulary properly, then listen to the audio as many times as necessary until you feel confident that you are pronouncing them well.

This may be a little tricky in the beginning, but as you keep reading the book, you will pronounce them with ease and natural.

The below example is how all the vocabulary and sentences will be provided in this book.

Example:

How are you doing?

tl: nuvvu yela chesththunnavu

lit: you how are doing.

In Detail: nuvvu - you, yela - how, chesththunnavu - doing (present tense).

Transliteration (tl) - This is the transliteration of the Telugu script; in simple words, this is how a Telugu pronunciation would be if it's written in Telugu.

Literally (lit) - Since the word order for many sentences is different compared to English, I have provided the literal translation of the Telugu script.

Note: Most English speakers have different English accent based on where they are from, e.g., An American person, a British person, an Indian, and an Australian will have a different English accent. Hence, they will have different transliteration based on their accent. The transliteration that I have provided is based on a neutral accent which is easier to follow and provides a common ground for all the English speakers irrespective of their accent. If you feel that the transliteration provided is not close to your accent please don't worry, just continue and keep practicing the pronunciation. Eventually, you will get the hang of it, and you will follow my transliteration; as there is an audio to help you out as well with the pronunciation of every vocabulary and sentence.

Note: Dear Linguistics and other IPA pronunciation experts, please accept my apologies for not using IPA pronunciation in this book. This book is targeted for those who are new to learning a language, and I intend to make their life as easy as possible by being an invisible teacher next to them and guiding them as much as possible.

3) I have created many courses in the mobile and desktop application (memrise) to help you to learn Telugu Alphabets, Vocabulary, Verbs, Verb conjugation, etc. A separate section will be provided to help you in installing and using this application.

4) You are not expected to learn all the vocabularies before you begin; it is recommended to learn vocabularies little by little. But you are expected to learn and memorize pronouns and their suffixes, Verbs and their conjugated forms as they are frequently used throughout the book.

5) Keys to the exercises are given at the end of every lesson.

6) Please try to understand every part given in the book, a lot of effort has been put into this book to explain them in great detail with lots of examples because a concept or a part that is being mentioned in one chapter will not be repeated in other chapter. So, I expect you to put a lot of effort into understanding what's given in the book rather than memorizing the Telugu words.

7) I have explained most of the rules in Telugu grammar and made patterns in the Telugu grammar for better understanding and to speak easily in this book. But there are few exceptions, and since you are learning spoken Telugu, colloquially some letters have been changed for ease of pronunciation by the Telugu people, and I don't have a pattern or rule to explain them. You just have to learn them and use them as it is. When you see a word or a suffix which doesn't follow the rule that I gave, then it is like it is, this suffix which didn't follow the rule is an exception, and you just have to learn them as it is.

What to Expect from the Book and How This Book is designed?

Telugu language is a lot different from English, be it the script or the grammar, etc. There are lots of rules and grammars involved in the language. If you were to learn everything before speaking the language, then you will have to learn forever. So, I have taken some important grammar topics, words, and suffixes and explained them in great detail, so that you can start speaking in Telugu.

Guarantee:

I can Guarantee you that, if you read this book with complete focus, motivation and willingness to put effort into learning and understanding the grammar given here and memorize the Telugu words and suffixes, then you will definitely be able to make sentences in Telugu consisting of 3-6 words, which you can use to make small talk with native speakers of Telugu.

This book is designed in a step by step practical approach to get you to start speaking in Telugu.

After completing Lesson 1, you will be able to understand about the pronunciation of the Telugu transliteration and how to pronounce them; Lesson 2 is to help you with vocabularies that you will come across in the following Lessons.

After completing Lesson 3 and Lesson 5, you will be able to understand the pronouns and their suffixes and when to use them.

After completing Lesson 5 and Lesson 6 you would have memorized around 70 verbs and their conjugation in all three tense. Now you will be able to make 3-word sentences in Telugu using your Verb conjugation knowledge and to use command and request in Telugu. Now you have reached 50% of your goals in this book.

After completing Lesson 9 you will be able to effectively use the cases as per your needs and make much more sentences in Telugu. With cases in your arsenal, you will be able to make sentences containing 4-5 words. Now you have reached 75% of your goals in this book.

After completing Lesson 10 and Lesson 11 you will be able to negate a sentence and you will be able to make much more sentences in Telugu. With Lesson 12, you will be able to make sentences with adverbs and adjectives. Now you have reached 100% of your goals in this book. You will be able to make a sentence in Telugu with 3-6 words.

After completing this book, you could take classes and learn more Telugu from Aswani Kopparapu (agoparaju.2009@gmail.com) or speak with a native Telugu speaker or listen to Telugu music and watch Telugu movies or do all the above to improve your fluency in Telugu.

Colloquial Telugu v/s Old Telugu.

The spoken Telugu that we speak now (Colloquial) is a little different from what we used to speak 30 - 40 years back; a lot has been changed for the ease of speaking faster and for easy pronunciation. Most of the native speakers nowadays will not pronounce the last letter of many of the Telugu words and they tend to change some letters in the Telugu words to make it easier for pronunciation.

Variation in Dialects.

Similar to English (American vs. British vs. Australian English Accents), Telugu also has various dialects; the Telugu spoken in Hyderabad is a bit different from the Telugu spoken in Vijayawada, even the Telugu spoken in different parts of Andhra Pradesh and Telangana (e.g., Visakhapatnam, Nellore, etc.) will have their own dialects but the basic Telugu is still the same. Don't you worry, because any individual who can speak Telugu fluently will be able to understand any dialect.

This book is mainly focusing on the 20th century spoken Telugu; I have tried my best to form grammars and rules to help you learn spoken Telugu with ease.

Andhra Telugu v/s Telangana Telugu

The Telugu spoken in the state of Andhra Pradesh and Telangana have slightly different dialects, again similar to the example of English spoken in the United states and the United Kingdom. So, if you are fluent in Telugu, then you will be able to understand the Telugu native speakers and the Telugu native speakers will be able to understand you perfectly irrespective of the accent.

Something else you can do apart from reading this book to boost your Telugu learning and becoming fluent in Telugu.

1) Entertainment: Telugu Cinema is a vast entertainment industry. Every year around 200 plus movies get released, and we have movies of every genre -- Action, comedy, romance, Thriller, etc. If you think that all we do in Indian movies is dance and sing, then you are absolutely wrong. There are few movies which do that, but there are many movies which showcase the society and have a very good story in it.

To watch Telugu movies, you can go and register on any of the websites mentioned below; they provide lots of Telugu movies with English subtitles. Please check the reviews and watch because some movies are not worth watching at all.

https://www.einthusan.tv

http://www.hotstar.com/

Some of the movies that I would personally recommend: Baahubali, Rangasthalam, Bharat Ane Nenu, Arjun Reddy, Midhunam, Srimanthadu. Manam etc.

2) Music: Telugu music has a long tradition and history going back thousands of years. Music is an essential aspect of the culture to the Telugu people. Telugu film music is widely known for its innovation and eclecticism. Scores may showcase blends of Carnatic, Western and other instruments, with a range of melodic and rhythmic patterns.

Below are some links where you can listen to Telugu music; you can even download the app gaana or saavn in your apple or android phones to listen to Telugu music. Telugu has millions of music with lots of varieties to offer.

https://gaana.com/playlist/gaana-dj-telugu-top-20

https://www.saavn.com/Telugu

http://gaana.com/album/Telugu

https://www.youtube.com/watch?v=hbsqjstbjy0

https://www.youtube.com/watch?v=ftVjT0tMHLQ

3) Practice with your Telugu friends and Family, if they have enough patience for it.

Guide on Installing the Memrise Application:

Memrise is a language learning platform with a website, iOS, and Android apps. Memrise specializes in combining memory techniques and entertaining content in order to make language learning recreational.

Steps to Create and Register in Memrise.

1) Go to the link www.decks.memrise.com

2) Click signup, register, and create a new account for yourself.

3) Go to the below-mentioned links and click the 'learn' button.

Telugu Vocabularies:

www.bit.ly/telugucourse

Telugu sentences:

www.bit.ly/telugucourse2

That's it, you can start learning Telugu vocabularies through memrise from Desktop.

To learn Memrise from your Android or Apple mobile, follow the steps below:

1) Go to Google play store or apple store

2) Search for the memrise app and click Install

3) Provide your user credentials

4) Since you have already learned the course on desktop before installing the app, it will be automatically added to your account, and it will get displayed on your mobile, so you don't have to search for the course again.

Have fun learning Telugu through memrise!

Downloading the Audio Files for This Book.

Audio has been provided for every part of the Telugu script in the book, please listen to them while learning this book; it will be beneficial for your pronunciation. How to download these audio files are explained below. The audio files are categorized through page numbers and their lesson name.

1) Go to the below link.

www.bit.ly/teluguaudio

2a) Left click on the file provided, they are similar to the image below.

3) Click the 'Download' button to download the audio file.

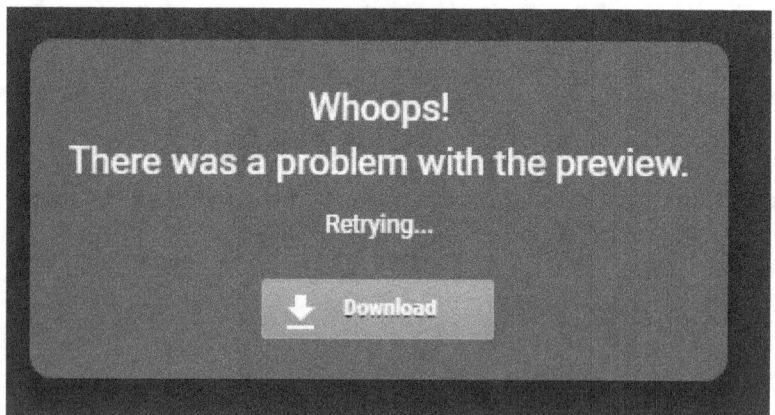

2b) as an alternative you can click on the 'download all' button on the right top corner of the page to download the audio files.

4) The files will be in WinRAR format, so you will have to unzip the files to access the audio.

For more information, contact me through my email id: indianlanguages101@gmail.com

How to Write in Telugu on a Keyboard

There are multiple ways to use Telugu keyboard on your computer; you can use any method that suits your need.

This method is pretty straight forward, but you need to have an internet connection to copy and paste the Telugu script every single time.

Step 1: Go to the website mentioned below:

http://telugu.changathi.com/

Step 2: You will see a screen where you can type the English transliteration as I did.

Step 3: Once you type the transliteration, press the space bar and the transliteration will get converted into a Telugu script.

Step 4: If this is not the desired Telugu script, then you can press the backspace key twice and you will be provided with a drop-down menu to choose the desired Telugu script from.

Step 5: Now you can copy and paste the Telugu script in Skype, MS word, or anywhere else you want.

If you need any further assistance, you can email me at indianlanguages101@gmail.com

LESSON 1: PRONUNCIATION TIPS

As I have mentioned to you earlier, since this book is not provided with the Telugu script and everything has been transliterated into English, the pronunciation is going to be quite difficult since English doesn't have an extensive arsenal of scripts like "Greek or Latin". So, I have provided you with audios for most of the Telugu transliterations in this book, provided you will also find the below pronunciations tips to be very helpful.

The below will describe how to pronounce these letters when you see them in the Telugu transliteration.

1. 'e': unlike English, irrespective of where this letter has been placed in the transliterated Telugu word, you should always pronounce it like the alphabet 'a' in English. Example: mercury, sediment, empire, etc.

Note: In English, under phonetics, you will have specific rules to pronounce the alphabets differently. Example: 'empire' and 'value', here both words include of the alphabet 'e', but you will pronounce the alphabet 'e' differently in both of these words. But in our Telugu transliteration in this book, you will always pronounce the letter 'e' the same as pronouncing the letter 'e' in 'empire'.

Example: Telugu word 'meemu' (we) should not be pronounced as 'miimu' (Incorrect), As I mentioned before, the pronunciation of the letter 'e' may change in English based on the phonetics but here in Telugu transliteration you will always pronounce the letter 'e' the same.

2. 'i': Similar to the above situation, irrespective of where this letter has been placed in the transliterated Telugu word, you should always pronounce it like the alphabet 'e' in English. **Example:** India, Impress, Image etc.

Example: Telugu word 'aavida' (she) should be pronounced properly. I am sorry, I find it very difficult to explain this to you through writing. For this chapter, please refer to the audio for better explanation and pronunciation of this word to get a much clearer understanding. As I mentioned earlier, the pronunciation of the letter 'i' may change in English based on the phonetics, but here in Telugu transliteration you will always pronounce the letter 'i' similar to the letter 'I' in 'India'.

3. Whenever you add a suffix to a Telugu word and the word ends with the letter 'u', then most of the time you will remove the letter 'u' while adding the suffix.

Example: thinu + aa + nu = thinnaanu (I ate)

As you saw in the example cited above, I skipped the letter 'u' while conjugating. If you ask me why I did that, what's the reason behind it? The answer would be to help you to pronounce the sentence with ease.

For example: Try pronouncing the same without removing the letter 'u'.

Example: thinu + aa + nu = thinnuaanu (I ate) (incorrect)

When you pronounced 'thinnaanu' and 'thinnuaanu', you would have recognized that the first one was much easier to pronounce, that's the very reason why we skip the letter 'u'. There are few exceptions, but 90% of the time you will remove the letter 'u' when you add a suffix to the word. Always remember that whenever you struggle a lot to pronounce a word in Telugu that means that you are making some mistakes. Telugu language is designed in such a manner that you should be able to pronounce the sentences with ease.

The above situation is sometimes even applicable for letters like 'e', 'i' and 'o'.

4. There are some words in Telugu which starts with the letter 'e', most of them are actually question words, e.g. 'evaru' (who), and there are few other words as well. Most of the time, especially when we are talking faster, we tend to use a tinge of 'y' before the letter 'e' when we pronounce a word which begins with the letter 'e'. That's why, for every word which starts with the letter 'e' in Telugu, I have added the letter 'y' before it. Please keep in mind that the letter 'y' should sound softly when you pronounce such words.
e.g., I have mentioned 'evaru' as 'yevaru' (who) in this book. When you say this word, soften the letter 'y'. It should be as subtle as possible.

5. Telugu is a completely new language for you, and if you are a native English speaker, then you are probably not used to the kind of pronunciation that we use in Telugu.
But don't worry, with practice you will get the Telugu pronunciation quickly, and I am going to help you with that.

In the below tables, I am going to give you a set of vowels and compound letters used in the Telugu language. I don't expect you to memorize these letters; I just want you to listen to the audio file that I have provided and repeat these letters after me and practice pronouncing them. You may make mistakes, but it doesn't matter; keep practicing, and you don't have to be perfect. Even if you are able to pronounce these letters perfectly around 70%, then that's good enough because you will be practicing them again and again through Telugu words and sentences in this whole book.

As mentioned earlier in points 1 & 2, the pronunciation of the letters 'i' and 'e' will be fixed in this book, and it's quite different from the way we use these letters in English. The vowels table given below will further help you to get a good understanding of how the pronunciation of these letters work. Please practice them so that you will be able to pronounce the Telugu letters correctly.

a) There are 16 vowels in Telugu language, and they are further classified into short and long vowels. Please refer to the below table for their pronunciation.

Vowels	Types	Pronunciation equivalent in English
a	Short vowel	As the sound of '**a**' in '**a**rrive' or '**a**rray'
aa	Long vowel	As the sound of '**aa**' in 'baz**aa**r'.
i	Short vowel	As the sound of 'i' in 'kick', 'sick'.
ii	Long vowel	As the sound of '**ii**' in 'sk**ii**ng' and as the sound of "**ee**" in 'd**ee**p', 'sl**ee**p'.
u	Short vowel	As the sound of '**u**' in 'p**u**t', 'p**u**ll'.
uu	Long vowel	As the sound of '**oo**' in 's**oo**n', 'm**oo**n', as the sound of '**u**' in 'tr**u**e', 'br**u**te'
ru	Short vowel	As the sound of '**ru**' in '**ru**pee'
ruu	Long vowel	As the sound of '**ru**' in '**ru**ral'.
e	Short vowel	As the sound of '**e**' in '**e**ntry', '**e**nd', '**e**xit' or as the sound of '**a**' in 't**a**me', 'c**a**ke'.
ee	Long vowel	As the sound of '**ay**' in 'del**ay**'.
ai	Long vowel	As the sound of '**I**' in 'iron', 'item', 'idea'.
o	Short vowel	As the sound of '**o**' in '**o**mit', 'sl**o**w'.
oo	Long vowel	As the sound of '**o**' in 'p**o**le' and as the sound of oa in 'c**oa**l'.
au	Long vowel	As the sound of '**ow**' in 'c**ow**', 'h**ow**', 'n**ow**'.
am		As the sound of '**m**' in sarcas**m**
aha		As the sound of '**ha**' in "nama**ha**"

There are two more vowels called 'lu' and 'loo', which were removed in modern Telugu. So, I have removed them from the above table as well.

b) There are a huge number of Telugu compound letter scripts. Since we are only practicing for pronouncing the Telugu letter, I have removed most of the Telugu scripts and mentioned only the scripts which we would mostly use in our book. Please listen to the audio and practice them as much as possible. As mentioned earlier, you don't have to perfect them, even if you achieve 70% perfection, its more than enough for this book.

1	ka	kaa	ki	kii	ku	kuu	kru	kruu	ke	kee	kai	ko	koo	kau	kam	kaha
2	kha	khaa	khi	khii	khu	khuu	khru	khruu	khe	khee	khai	kho	khoo	khau	kham	khaha
3	ga	gaa	gi	gii	gu	guu	gru	gruu	ge	gee	gai	go	goo	gau	gam	gaha
4	gha	ghaa	ghi	ghii	ghu	ghuu	ghru	ghruu	ghe	ghee	ghai	gho	ghoo	ghau	gham	ghaha
5	cha	chaa	chi	chii	chu	chuu	chru	chruu	che	chee	chai	cho	choo	chau	cham	chaha
6	ja	jaa	ji	jii	ju	juu	jru	jruu	je	jee	jai	jo	joo	jau	jam	jaha
7	ta	taa	ti	tii	tu	tuu	tru	truu	te	tee	tai	to	too	tau	tam	taha
8	tha	thaa	thi	thii	thu	thuu	thru	thruu	the	thee	thai	tho	thoo	thau	tham	thaha
9	da	daa	di	dii	du	duu	dru	druu	de	dee	dai	do	doo	dau	dam	daha
10	dha	dhaa	dhi	dhii	dhu	dhuu	dhru	dhruu	dhe	dhee	dhai	dho	dhoo	dhau	dham	dhaha
11	na	naa	ni	nii	nu	nuu	nru	nruu	ne	nee	nai	no	noo	nau	nam	naha
12	pa	paa	pi	pii	pu	puu	pru	pruu	pe	pee	pai	po	poo	pau	pam	paha
13	pha	phaa	phi	phii	phu	phuu	phru	phruu	phe	phee	phai	pho	phoo	phau	pham	phaaha
14	ba	baa	bi	bii	bu	buu	bru	bruu	be	bee	bai	bo	boo	bau	bam	baha
15	bha	bhaa	bhi	bhii	bhu	bhuu	bhru	bhruu	bhe	bhee	bhai	bho	bhoo	bau	bham	bhaha
16	ma	maa	mi	mii	mu	muu	mru	mruu	me	mee	mai	mo	moo	mau	mam	maha
17	ya	yaa	yi	yii	yu	yuu	yru	yruu	ye	yee	yai	yo	yoo	yau	yam	yaha
18	ra	raa	ri	rii	ru	ruu	rru	rruu	re	ree	rai	ro	roo	rau	ram	raha
19	la	laa	li	lii	lu	luu	lru	lruu	le	lee	lai	lo	loo	lau	lam	laha
20	va	vaa	vi	vii	vu	vuu	vru	vruu	ve	vee	vai	vo	voo	vau	vam	vaha
21	sa	saa	si	sii	su	suu	sru	sruu	se	see	sai	so	soo	sau	sam	saha
22	La	Laa	Li	Lii	Lu	Luu	Lru	Lruu	Le	Lee	Lai	Lo	Loo	Lau	Lam	Laha
23	sha	shaa	shi	shii	shu	shuu	shru	shruu	she	shee	shai	sho	shoo	shau	sham	shaha

Note: As you saw in the above compound letters chart, there are two different types of 'la' in row 19 and 22. One is with small letters, and the other one is with capital letters. In proper Telugu, both are indeed different, and should be pronounced differently.

Don't worry too much about the above point. Since you are a beginner, I would recommend you skip the capital "L" form for the time being; whenever you see them just pronounce them the same way as the small 'l' is pronounced. But as you progress and you become better in Telugu, start pronouncing the capital 'L' and small 'l' differently, because this will show others how good you are in Telugu.

Picture representation for pronunciation:

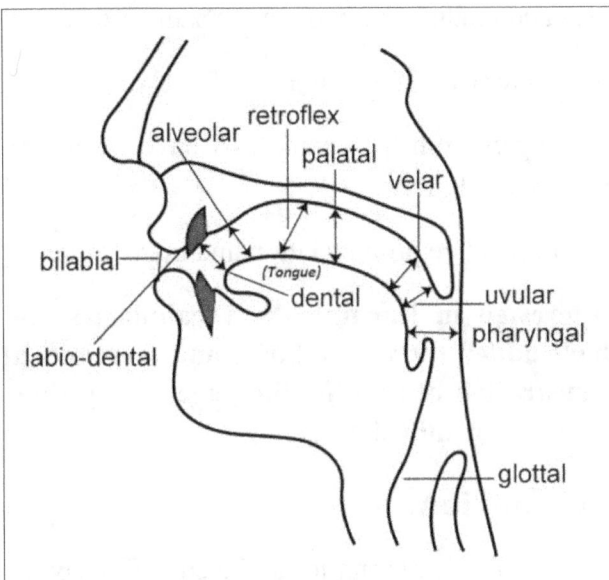

Pronunciation guide for 'la':

As alveolar lateral, the tip of your tongue curves back a little and moves further in front of the alveolar region of the mouth and released. This one is straight forward and easy to pronounce.

Pronunciation guide for 'La':

In order to pronounce this letter, the tongue has to be folded upward a little bit more than what you did for 'la' and try not to touch the palatal or retroflex while releasing your tongue and pronounce the letter 'La'. If you touch the palatal or retroflex while pronouncing, then you will pronounce 'la' instead of 'La'. This is the difference in pronouncing 'la' and 'La'.

LESSON 2: VOCABULARIES, SENTENCES AND ROLE PLAY SCENARIOS

Telugu Vocabularies:

Kindly find tables with useful Telugu vocabularies at the end of this book that is being used in this book. I would recommend you memorize these vocabularies in your free time either by using the memrise app or by using the traditional method of reading and memorizing from the book. But don't spend too much time on it, maybe around 15 minutes every day will be good.

The advantage of memorizing these vocabularies and reading the book at the same are many:

1) You will be able to recollect the vocabularies while reading the book.

2) You will be able to make multiple sentences apart from the examples I have given you because you have lots of vocabularies in your arsenal right now

3) Much easier to do the exercise from the book, to practice pronunciation and many more.

Note: Since some of you might not be interested in learning the vocabularies and sentences before learning the grammar. I have added the vocabularies and sentences at the end of the book to save you from the frustration of flipping the pages every time, especially for those who are reading the book using Kindle device.

Telugu Sentences & Role play scenarios:

Kindly find tables with useful Telugu sentences and role play scenarios at the end of this book.

Note: It is advisable for the learners not to concentrate in learning sentences before learning other lessons in this book because Telugu grammar is a bit different from English grammar. If you look at the Telugu sentences before learning Telugu grammar, you will get confused and find it difficult to comprehend the Telugu sentences. Whereas, when you learn Telugu grammar and then look at these sentences, then you will be able to understand and learn the sentences well.

The above statement is just a suggestion, as this is the best way to learn Telugu in my opinion. But there are some exceptions as well.

1. You could also learn these Telugu sentences simultaneously along with other lessons (Telugu grammar), this would help you to understand Telugu grammar better and at the same time your Telugu vocabularies will get better.

2. Some of you might just want to learn few sentences in Telugu language to practice it with native Telugu speakers and you might not be interested in Telugu grammar at all. This table is for you as well.

LESSON 3: SUFFIXES IN TELUGU

The Telugu language is made up of lots of suffixes; these suffixes represent tenses, cases, pronoun, number, gender, adverbs, prepositions, etc. Suffixes are an important part of the Telugu language; Once you have mastered the suffixes, then it's much easier to speak in Telugu. This means, you have lots of possibilities and options to form sentences in Telugu using these suffixes.

An example of suffix in English: In English, we use the suffix '-ist' to indicate 'the one who does', for example: chemist, activist, alchemist, biologist, etc. Here we add the suffix '-ist' at the end of each profession to point out the person who does it.

Suffixes also serve the purpose of shortening some words and adding them to other words.

For Instance, In English, we usually add the prepositions before a noun or the pronoun, e.g. 'in the book', 'with him', 'to the office', 'for her', etc. Whereas in Telugu we will add these prepositions in the form of a suffix and add it to the word itself (like a word ending); these are called case endings.

Interrogative Suffix (-aa)

To make a sentence as a question in Telugu, you can either add a questioner word like 'yenti' (what) or you can add an interrogative suffix:

1. To the end of the sentence or 2. To any word (except modifier of a noun) which is questioned in the sentence.

Let's take a noun, for example 'pusthakam': in order to make this a question, all you have to do is add the Interrogative Suffix 'aa' at the end of the noun.

pusthakam + '-aa' ('Interrogative suffix') = pusthakamaa (is this a book?)

Let's take a pronoun, for example 'athanu' (he): in order to make this a question, all you have to do is add the Interrogative Suffix 'aa' at the end of the pronoun.

athanu + '-aa' ('Interrogative suffix') = athanaa (is that him?)

Let's take a simple sentence, for example 'athanu thinnaadu' (he ate): in order to make this a question, all you have to do is add the Interrogative Suffix 'aa' at the end of the pronoun.

athanu (thinnaadu + '-aa' (Interrogative suffix)) = athanu thinnaadaa? (did he eat?)

Another example 'miiru thintaaru' (You will eat): in order to make this a question, all you have to do is add the Interrogative Suffix '-aa' at the end of the pronoun.

miiru (thintaaru + '-aa' ('Interrogative suffix')) = miiru thintaaraa? (Will you eat?)

Note: If the name of a person ends with the letter 'a', then you should add the interrogative suffix '-na' instead of '-aa' because adding interrogative suffix '-aa' to the name would make it much more difficult to pronounce and you will struggle a lot. That's why, whenever a name ends with the letter 'a' and you want to add an interrogative suffix to it to make it as a question then you should simply add a word 'na' instead of the suffix '-aa'. The word 'na' at the end of the sentence will give the same effect as adding the suffix '-aa' to the sentence.

Example: (Raja = this is an Indian name of a male person)

nenu raja (I am raja)

Let's say you need to change the above sentence to a question without the use of a question word, then you would apply the method given below.

Correct sentence: nenu raja na? (Am I raja?)

Incorrect sentence: nenu rajaaa?

Why is the above sentence incorrect? Just try pronouncing the incorrect sentence, and you will find its extremely hard to pronounce it and that's why we use the word 'na' here instead of simply adding the suffix '-aa' to the end of the word.

Politeness in Telugu:

1) The suffix '-andi' brings politeness to the word. The suffix '-andi' may exist in the word itself or it can be added as a suffix, whenever you add this suffix to a word it brings politeness.

Example:

a) cheppu (say, tell)

cheppu + '-andi' = cheppandi (please tell)

The suffix '-andi' when added in a word automatically includes please in a sentence.

b) ivvu (to give)

ivvu + '-andi' = ivvandi (please give)

c) raayi (to write)

raayi + '-andi' = raayandi (please write).

d) veLLu (to go)

veLLu + '-andi' = veLLandi (please go).

2) The word 'gaaru' is used in Telugu when you want to address a person with respect. It is similar to 'Mr' and 'Ms' in English but the only difference here is, 'gaaru' is used often in Telugu than 'Mr' amd 'Ms' in English.

Example:

a) Raju ('Raju' is a common male Indian name)

Raju + gaaru = Raju gaaru (Mr. Raju)

b) Peter

Peter + gaaru = Peter gaaru (Mr. Peter)

c) Mary

Mary + gaaru = Mary gaaru (Ms. Mary)

d) Lakshmi ('Lakshmi' is a common male Indian name)

Lakshmi + gaaru = Lakshmi gaaru (Ms. Lakshmi)

Question Words in Telugu:

Question words in Telugu can be placed in more than one position in a sentence. Most of the Question words start with the letter 'ye'.

The following table will give you a list of Telugu question words.

Question words	English
yenti?	What?
yendhuku?	Why?
yevaru?	Who?
yekkada?	Where?
yeppudu?	When?
yeedhi?	Which (noun)?
ye?	Which (adjective)?
yela?	How?
yenni?	How many?
yentha?	How much?

LESSON 4: PRONOUNS

List of Pronouns:

	Singular		Plural	
	Nominative	**Possessive**	**Nominative**	**Possessive**
First person	nenu (I)	naa (my)	manamu (we) (listener included)	mana (our) (listener included)
			meemu (we) (listener not included)	maa (our) (listener not included)
Second person	nuvvu (you)	nii (your)	miiru (You) (Polite)	mii (your) (polite)
	miiru (You) (Polite)	mii (your) (polite)		
Third person	athanu/vaadu (he)	athani (his)	vaaLLu (they-human) (polite)	vaari (their-human) (polite)
	aayana (he) (polite)	aayana (his) (polite)		
	aame (she)	aame (her)		
	aavida (she) (polite)	aavida (her) (polite)		
	adhi (that) idhi (this), both the word also means it.	dhaani (that) dhiini(this), both the word also means it.	avi (those) ivi (these)	vaati (those) viiti (these)

Pronouns in Telugu are almost similar to English pronouns with some exceptions. Pronouns are divided into three 'persons': first person (the speaker), second person (the listener), and third person (the person spoken about). In Telugu, pronouns agree and represent a Person, Number, and Gender (PNG).

Person - First person or Second person or Third person; Number - Singular or Plural; Gender - Male or Female.

Nominative: It is the subject of the sentence and a basic form of a noun without any suffix being added to it. In Telugu nominative usually refers to an action. e.g., 'neenu thintunnaanu' (I am eating), 'nuvvu parigeduthunnaavu' (you are running).

a) You would have noticed in the above chart that Telugu, unlike English, has two forms of 'you'. 'nuvvu' is an impolite form of 'you' while 'miiru' is a polite form of 'you' and can be used for both singular and plural. Whenever you are in doubt on which one to use, always use 'miiru' (polite form of 'you').

b) The third person pronoun is divided into three genders: "human masculine 'he', human feminine 'she', and neutral 'it'". We have polite forms for singular 'he' and 'she' in Telugu; the polite form of singular 'he' is 'aayana', and the polite form of singular 'she' is 'aavida'. 'aavida' is also used as 'they' (plural form) when you are referring to a group of people.

This polite form is usually used when you are referring to elders, superiors, and strangers. The impolite form 'nuvvu' (you), 'athanu/vaadu' (he), and 'aame' (she) is usually used when you are referring to someone younger than you and with someone whom you have a close relationship with. e.g., Friends.

c) Unlike in English, we have two different corresponding pronouns for 'we' in Telugu.

One is 'manamu' (we) (listener included); this includes the person with whom you are speaking to as well.

Example: let's say you are telling me 'manamu shopki veLthunnamu' (we are going to the shop), then it means that "yourself, myself, and a bunch of others are going to the shop"

The other one is 'meemu' (we) (listener not included); this does not include the person with whom you are speaking to.

Example: let's say you are telling me 'meemu shopki veLthunnamu' (we are going to the shop), then it means that "only yourself and a bunch of others are going to the beach" and you are simply telling this to me as an information.

Proximate and Remote Pronoun (demonstrative pronouns):

In Telugu, we use separate words when referring to a third person Proximate (nearby) and remote (far away), these are also called demonstrative pronouns.

Example: 'aayana Tom' (he is Tom); here you are referring to the person ' Tom' who is far away from you (e.g. Tom is sitting a meter away from you). 'iiyana Tom' (he is tom); here you are referring to the person 'tom' who is nearby (e.g. Tom is sitting next to you). To make it easier for you to remember, if the word starts with 'I', then it means it is proximate (nearby); if the word starts with 'a' then it is remote (far away).

	Singular	Plural
	Nominative/case form	**Nominative/case form**
Third Person Proximate	ithanu/viidu (he)	viiLLu (they)
	iiyana (he - polite)	
	iime (she)	
	iivida (she - polite)	
	idhi (this, it)	ivi (these)
Third Person Remote	athanu/vaadu (he)	vaaLLu (they)
	aayana (he - polite)	
	aame (she)	
	aavida (she - polite)	
	adhi (that, it)	avi (those)

Note: I have explained most of the rules in Telugu grammar and made patterns in the Telugu grammar for better understanding and to speak easily in this book.

But there are few exceptions, and since you are learning spoken Telugu, colloquially some letters have been changed for ease of pronunciation by the Telugu speaking people. Some grammar topics are so complicated that they have different suffix depending on the verb and verb endings, but they are rarely used and I don't have a pattern or rules to explain them. You just have to learn them and use them as it is.

When you see a word or a suffix which doesn't follow the rule that I gave, then please listen to the audio for that word or suffix. If it is the same in the audio as well, then probably it is like it is and you just have to learn them as it is.

Demonstrative and Interrogative Pronoun:

With reference to the above, there is another set of interrogative pronouns. The interrogative pronoun begins with the letter 'ye'. These are used as a question word 'which' in relation to a set of person who is already mentioned or a thing or day etc.

	Demonstrative		Interrogative
	Proximate	**Remote**	
Masculine	ithanu (he)	athanu (he)	'yevaru' (Who?)
Feminine	iime (she)	aame (she)	
Masculine	iiyana (he - polite)	aayana (he - polite)	
Feminine	iivida (she - polite)	aavida (she - polite)	
Plural	viiLLu (they)	vaaLLu (they)	
Plural	ivi (these)	avi (those)	yevi (Which ones?)
Things/ Animals	idhi (this - noun)	adhi (that - noun)	yedhi (Which? - noun)
Things/ Animals	i (this - adjective)	a (that - adjective)	ye (Which? - adjective)
	ikkada (here)	akkada (there)	yekkada (Where?)
	ippudu (this time, now)	appudu (that time, then)	yeppudu (Which time?/At what time? When?)
	intha (this much)	antha (that much)	yentha (How much?)
	inni (this many)	anni (that many)	yenni? (How many?)
	ila (like this, this way/manner)	ala (like that, that way/manner)	yela (Like how? In what way/manner?)
	'ivvaala / i roju' means 'this day or today',	'a roju' means 'that's day,	'ye roju' means 'which day?'
	indhuku (For this reason)	andhuku (For that reason)	yendhuku? (For what reason?)
	itu vaipu (this side)	atu vaipu (that side)	yetu vaipu? (Which side?)

Difference between 'i' (this - adjective), 'a' (that - adjective), 'ye' (which? - adjective) and 'idhi' (this - noun) 'adhi' (that - noun) 'yedhi' (which? - noun):

As you have seen in the above table, 'i' and 'idhi' both means 'this'. The difference here is, when you use 'i', then an adjective should come next to it, when you use 'idhi' then a noun should come after it. 'idhi' is like "pointing at something (person or object)", whereas 'i' is like defining an object or a person.

Example:

a) **i** pusthakam (this book) - here you are just pointing at a book that is near you. (For example: you are in a book shop and you point your finger asking for a particular book)

b) **idhi** pusthakam (this is a book) - here you are explaining to someone (maybe a kid) that 'this is a book', which is also nearby. (For example: you are explaining to a three-year-old kid that this is a book)

c) **a** pusthakam (that book) - here you are just pointing at a book which is far from you. This is the same as 'i' except that the one you are pointing at is far away from you.

d) **adhi** pusthakam (that is a book) - here you are explaining to someone (maybe a kid) 'that is a book', which is also far away from you. This is same as the 'idhi' except that the one you are explaining about/defining is far away from you.

e) **ye** pusthakam? (Which book?) - Here you are pointing to a bunch of books and questioning 'which book'. (For example: you are in a book shop and the shop-keeper points to a bunch of books in his shelf and questions you, which book do you want?)

f) **yedhi** pusthakam? (Which is a book?) - Here you are pointing to a group of objects and questioning 'which is a book'. (For example: you are opening your friend's cupboard with lots of things in it and question him which one of this here is a book?).

Note: Most of the interrogative pronouns have already been provided under the heading "Question words and Interrogative Suffix 'aa' earlier.

Exercises:

A) Match the following Telugu pronoun in the first column with the appropriate English meaning in the second column.

1	mii	a	I
2	athanu	b	you (informal)
3	aame	c	you (polite) (singular)
4	meemu	d	he
5	adhi	e	she
6	nenu	f	he (polite)
7	aavida	g	she (polite)
8	manamu	h	that
9	miiru	i	this
10	maa	j	my
11	aayana	k	your (informal)
12	nuvvu	l	your (polite) (singular)
13	nenu	m	we (listener included)
14	nuvvu	n	we (listener excluded)
15	idhi	o	our (listener included)
16	mana	p	our (listener excluded)

B) Choose the correct answer by selecting the right pronoun.

e.g. _____ Tom.

a. athanu   b. aame   c. adhi

The right answer is: 'athanu' Tom (he is Tom), since Tom is a male person name.

1. _____ Mary.

a. athanu   b. aame   c. adhi

2. _____ Dog.

a. athanu   b. aame   c. adhi

3. _____ (polite) Tom.

a. athanu   b. aame   c. aayana

4. _____ (polite) Mary.

a. aavida   b. aame   c. aayana

5. _____ (peru) (name) Jack.

a. naa   b. adhi   c. aame

6. _____peru Peter.

a. nii   b. adhi   c. aame

C) Now try to use the above exercise as reference and change the same sentence that you formed into a question

Example: my - 'naa peru raja' (my name is raja)

Now change the above into a question: "naa peru raja na?" (Is my name raja?)

1. Your

2. Her

3. His

4. That's

5. Its

6. She (polite)

7. He (polite)

D) Use a pronoun to point to a person's name mentioned below.

Masculine: Raja, Ram, Ramesh; Feminine: Mala, Lakshmi, Akila.

Example: I - 'nenu raja' (I am raja)

1. You

2. You (polite)

3. He

4. He (polite)

5. She

6. She (polite)

E) Introduce a person's name, using the word 'peru' (name) and the case form of a pronoun.

Example: my - 'naa peru raja' (my name is raja)

1. mii (your)

2. aame (her)

3. athanu (his)

4. dhaani (that's)

5. dhiini (it's)

6. aavida (she (polite))

7. aayana (he (polite))

F) Translate the English Question into Telugu Question.

Example: who is this boy? - 'i baaludu yevaru'

1. What is that?

2. What is this?

3. How many?

4. How much?

5. What time is it?

G) Choose the correct answer by selecting the right question word.

1. _____ Tomato?

a. yenni   b. yela   c. yeppudu

2. _____ veLthaaru (you will go)?

a. yeppudu   b. yedhi   c. yedhi

3. _____ veLthaaru (you will go)?

a. inni   b. yedhi   c. yela

4. _____ veLthaaru (you will go)?

a. yekkada   b. viiLLu   c. iiyana

5. _____ rupaayalu (rupees)?

a. yenni   b. yela   c. yeppudu

6. _____ veLthaaru (when will you go)?

a. yeppudu   b. a   c. idhi

H) Translate the following from English to Telugu.

Example: Which is a head - yedhi thala?

1. This is a boy.

2. This boy.

3. This a house.

4. Which house?

5. Which is a house?

6. Which boy?

7. That house.

8. Which vehicle?

9. That is a vehicle.

10 Which is a vehicle?

I) Translate the following from Telugu to English.

Example: idhi thala - This is a head, (Vocabulary: kukka = dog)

1. idhi kukka.

2. i kukka.

3. ye kukka.

4. yedhi kukka.

5. adhi kukka.

6. a kukka.

J) Match the following Telugu question words in the first column with the appropriate English meaning in the second column.

1.	yenti	a	How many?
2.	yendhuku	b	Where?
3.	yeme	c	Which man?
4.	yevaru	d	Which women?
5.	yekkada	e	Which (noun)?
6.	yeppudu	f	Which day?
7.	yedhi	g	What?
8.	ye	h	How?
9.	yela	i	Which (adjective)?
10.	yenni	j	Why?
11.	yentha	k	When?
12.	ye roju	l	How much?
13.	yee aayana	m	Who?

Solutions

Exercise A

1) l; 2) d; 3) e; 4) n; 5) h; 6) a; 7) g; 8) o; 9) c; 10) p; 11) f; 12) b; 13) j; 14) k; 15) i; 16) m.

Exercise B: 1) b; 2) c; 3) c; 4) a; 5) a; 6) a.

Note: In Exercise C, D, and E, you can use random names; I used the names randomly, that's all.

Exercise C

1) nii peru raja na? 2) aame peru mala na? 3) athani peru raja na?4) dhaani peru raja na? 5) dhiini peru raja na? 6) aavida peru mala na? 7) aayana peru raja na?

Exercise D

1) nuvvu raja. 2) miiru raam. 3) athanu rameesh. 4) aayana raja. 5) aame maalaa. 6) aavida agilaa.

Exercise E

1) mii peru raja 2) aame peru maalaa 3) athanu peru raja 4) dhaani peru tiger 5) dhiini peru raajaa 6) aavida peru maalaa 7) aayana peru raajaa.

Exercise F: 1) adhi yenti? 2) idhi yenti? 3) yenni? 4) yentha? 5) time yenti?

Exercise G: 1) a; 2) a; 3) c; 4) a; 5) a; 6) a.

Exercise H

1) idhi baaludu. 2) i baaludu. 3) idhi illu. 4) ye illu? 5) yedhi illu? 6) ye baaludu? 7) a illu. 8) ye vaahanam? 9) adhi vaahanam. 10) yedhi vaahanam?

Exercise I

1) This is a dog. 2) This dog. 3) Which dog? 4) What dog? 5) That dog. 6) That is a dog.

Exercise J

1) g; 2) j; 3) d; 4) m; 5) b; 6) k; 7) e; 8) i; 9) h; 10) a; 11) l; 12) f; 13) c.

LESSON 5: VERB CONJUGATION

Verb conjugation refers to how a verb changes to show a different person, tense, or number.

Review of Verb conjugation in English: In English, to conjugate a verb, it is necessary to adhere to the form below.

1. Person: In English, we have six different persons; first person singular (I), second person singular (you), third person singular (he/she/it/one) and we have to use them as it. A conjugated verb will always have a pronoun before it.

2. Tense: Verbs are also conjugated according to a tense; Verb tense shows when the action in a sentence is happening or happened or will happen (e.g., in the present, future, or past). Regular verbs follow a standard pattern as mentioned in the table below, and we have few irregular verbs that don't follow a standard pattern.

	Simple past	Simple present	Simple future	Present continuous
Regular	Cooked	Cook	Will cook	Cooking
Irregular	Ate	Eat	Will eat	Eating

Verb Conjugation in Telugu:

A conjugated verb in a sentence consists of three parts.

1. The root of the verb. e.g., thinu (to eat)

2. A suffix which indicates the tense, e.g., '-aa' (class 3: Past tense)

3. Another suffix which indicates the PNG (Person-Number-Gender) e.g., '-nu' (verb suffix of 'nenu')

thinu + '-aa' + nu = thinnaanu (I ate)

Note: The root of the verb, e.g., 'thinu', can occur on its own as an imperative form, which is simply to instruct someone to do something.

Verb conjugation in Telugu is different from English; the points listed below will explain those differences with examples.

1) Similar to English, we use pronouns which comes before a conjugated verb, adding to this we use a verb suffix as well which represents the PNG (Person Number Gender) like a pointer to the pronoun but this is optional in colloquial spoken Telugu.

Example:

Let's take the Pronoun: 'nenu' (I), verb: 'vinu' (to hear), Present tense suffix: '-taa', Verb suffix for 'nenu' which is '-nu'.

Using the above example, I will be able to form a sentence "I will hear".

nenu (pronoun 'I') + vinu (to hear) + taa (Future tense suffix) + nu (Verb suffix of 'nenu' (I))

When you combine all together, we will get 'nenu vintaanu'.

2) In Telugu, we use only present continuous tense; we don't have a separate present tense unlike English.

Tense	Example	Translation	Explanation
Past tense	nenu thinnaanu	I ate	You already finished the activity
Present continuous	nenu thintunnaanu	I am eating	The activity is still in progress
Present tense	nenu thintaanu	I eat	The activity may happen now within the next few minutes or today itself (present tense) or the activity may happen in the future (future tense)
Future tense	nenu thintaanu	I will eat	

Note: As shown in the above table, we don't have Simple present tense in Telugu instead we use simple future tense for simple present tense as well. The activity may take place in the present e.g., "by today or within the next few minutes", but nevertheless, you will refer to them using the future tense e.g., "nenu thintaanu (I eat/I will eat)" in Telugu. This may be a bit confusing for you initially as it's a lot different from English but in reality, it makes your life much easier as both present tense and future tense are referring to something which is going to happen and thus as a learner it makes your life much easier.

From here onwards I will be providing information only on Past, Present continuous, and future tense. Hence it is understood that you will use the future tense for the present tense as well in Telugu.

3) In Telugu, we don't use a separate word like 'are', 'is', 'am', 'was', 'has', 'have', 'were' when conjugating a verb like in English, depending on the 'person', 'tense', and 'context' it should be understood by the listener.

4) In Telugu, we use a suffix to represent whether the conjugated verb is in the past or present continuous or future tense. The verbs are split into different classes.

Note: About the verb classes, tense and tense suffixes will be explained in detail later in this chapter.

5) While conjugating a verb the 'verb root' is used and it usually changes depending on the verb root ending.

6) Note: The below explanations are just for your information only. Please read and understand them, but I would recommend you not to follow them unless you are fluent in Telugu. As long as you are not fluent in Telugu, you should always use the verb suffix.

Since the pronoun 'nenu' (I) already represents the suffix '-nu' (I), it is optional to use '-nu' in the sentence.'nenu vintaanu' and 'nenu vintaa' both means "I will hear". You should always use the pronoun e.g., 'nenu' when you conjugate a verb, it is mandatory, but when you do it, it is always optional to use the verb suffix e.g., '-nu', provided there is no suffix added next to it.

Example:

a) nenu vintaanu - I will hear

Since there is no suffix added to this sentence, you could also say 'nenu vintaa' and it means the same 'I will hear'. 'nenu vintaanu' and 'nenu vintaa' means exactly the same.

b) Now let's try to create the same sentence as a question by adding a suffix to it.

Correct sentence = nenu vintaanu + '-aa' = nenu vintaanaa (Will I hear?)

Incorrect sentence = nenu vintaa + '-aa' = nenu vintaaaa (Will I hear?)

As you see in the above sentences, the correct sentence looks proper and you can pronounce it fluently, while the incorrect sentence looks weird and you can't even pronounce it properly. So basically, whenever there is a suffix added to the verb suffix, you have no other choice but to use the verb suffix as well.

Now you may ask me "why is this happening?" In proper Telugu, we use the verb suffix mandatorily since it gives us a clear meaning. But as the time progressed, we started to ignore the verb suffix because we were able to understand the meaning of the verb conjugation even without the verb suffix since the sentence was accompanied by the pronoun. When there is a suffix which needs to be added to this conjugated verb, then we could no longer ignore this verb suffix because then we couldn't pronounce it properly or it sounds weird for us.

You don't have to worry about all these; I am just providing you with these as an information. What I would recommend to you is to use the verb suffix mandatorily, every single time.

Verb Suffixes:

Whenever a verb conjugation is referring to a pronoun, a suffix will be added to the verb that matches up with the subject of the sentence. This is applicable only for the nominative case pronouns; nominative case usually refers to an action. Each pronoun will be associated with a verb suffix. So, whenever a nominative case pronoun appears in a sentence, its corresponding verb suffix is added to the end of the verb.

This verb suffix is also known as a PNG suffix (Person-Number-Gender) as this agrees with all three of them.

The verb suffix table below shows Nominative case pronoun and their corresponding verb suffixes:

	Singular		Plural	
	Nominative	Suffix	Nominative	Suffix
First person	nenu (I)	-nu	manamu (we) (listener included)	-mu
			meemu (we) (listener not included)	-mu
Second person	nuvvu (you)	-vu	miiru (you) (polite)	-ru
	miiru (you) (polite)	-ru		
Third person	athanu/vaadu (he)	-du	vaaLLu (they-human) (polite)	-ru
	aayana (he) (polite)	-ru		
	aame (she)	-indhi / -thundhi		
	aavida (she) (polite)	-ru		
Things/ Animals	adhi (that) / idhi (this)	-indhi / -thundhi	avi (those) / ivi (these)	-yi

Note: The verb suffixes for "Person" given above will never change irrespective of which Tense you are using.

Tense:

As mentioned earlier, In Telugu, the Tenses are divided into three categories.

1. Past Tense (This relates to something that happened in the past).

2. Present continuous Tense (This relates to something that is in progress).

3. Future/Present Tense (This relates to something which will happen in the future, maybe in the next few minutes or at a later date).

In Present tense, when I say near future, it means it's going to happen today, tomorrow, or within a few days. We have the same concept in English as well, for example: 'I am going to the shop on Sunday' or 'Tom arrives tomorrow morning at six'. We have two possibilities here; you can either say 'I am going to the shop on Sunday' or 'I will go to the shop on Sunday', both indicate that you will go to the shop in the future but the tense can be present or future. In Telugu, this has been made much simpler; You use only Future tense for both Present and the future which is going to happen in a few minutes or at a later date.

If you find this to be more confusing, then don't worry; I will be explaining this in detail in this chapter with lots of examples as well.

1) The suffixes for the Past, Present continuous tense and Future tense are fixed for most of the verbs, there are few exceptions though.

Past Tense	Present continuous Tense	Future Tense
'-aa'	'-thunnaa'	'-thaa'

2) But as mentioned earlier, the verb root will change depending on the verb root ending. There are some similarities and some exceptions. It is very difficult to form a pattern; the best way to figure this out is to learn some verb conjugation. When you learn some verb conjugation, it will automatically get stuck to your brain on how the verb root will change and you will be able to conjugate from then on. In this book, I have given you many verb roots and their conjugations; try to learn them as much as possible and at one point you will be able to conjugate the verb by yourself, as there is a pattern but the pattern is very broad so we cannot put them in writing; which means you have to absorb them by learning and memorizing.

3) Try not to think too much and worry yourself that you have to understand and figure out everything that's being explained, especially with the Verb conjugation. I will be giving you lots of examples and explanations, at one point you will get the flow of it.

Example: The below table shows the verb conjugation of 'thinu' (to eat) in Past tense with verb suffix.

Pronoun	Verb root	Past Tense Suffix	Verb Suffix	Suffix combination with verb root	Past Tense	English Translation
nenu	thinu	-naa-	-nu	thinu+naa+nu	thinnaanu	I ate
nuvvu	thinu	-naa-	-vu	thinu+naa+vu	thinnaavu	You ate (informal/impolite)
miiru	thinu	-naa-	-ru	thinu+naa+ru	thinnaaru	You ate (formal/polite)
aayana	thinu	-naa-	-ru	thinu+naa+ru	thinnaaru	He ate (formal/polite)
aavida	thinu	-naa-	-ru	thinu+naa+ru	thinnaaru	She ate (formal/polite)
vaaLLu	thinu	-naa-	-ru	thinu+naa+ru	thinnaaru	They ate
athanu	thinu	-naa-	-du	thinu+naa+du	thinnaadu	He ate (informal/impolite)
meemu	thinu	-naa-	-mu	thinu+naa+mu	thinnaamu	we ate (listener inclusive)
manamu	thinu	-naa-	-mu	thinu+naa+mu	thinnaamu	we ate (listener exclusive)
aame/ adhi/idhi	thinu	-naa-	-indhi	thinnadhi	thinnadhi	She/that/this ate (informal/impolite)
avi/ivi	thinu	-naa-	-yi	thinu+naa+yi	thinnaayi	Those/These ate

1) There are two verb suffixes for the pronouns 'aame/adhi/idhi' (she (impolite)/that/this), this is because of the below mentioned reason.

a) We will use the verb suffix - '-indhi' usually in the past tense. There are some exceptions though but it is usually used in the past tense.

Example: 'adhi chadhivindhi' (It read) (Past tense)

b) We will use the verb suffix - '-thundhi' usually in the present continuous and future tense. There are some exceptions though but it is usually used in the present continuous and future tense.

Note: Whenever you conjugate 'aame/adhi/idhi' (she (impl)/that/this) then the conjugated form is the same for future and present continuous tense. This is an exception; this rule is only applicable for the pronoun 'aame/adhi/idhi' (she (impl)/that/this).

Example:

'aame chadhuvuthundhi' (she will read/she is reading) (Future tense and Present continuous tense)

'adhi chadhuvuthundhi' (It will read/it is reading) (Future tense and Present continuous tense)

'idhi chadhuvuthundhi' (It will read/it is reading) (Future tense and Present continuous tense)

Note: As you saw in the above example, I referred to both 'adhi' and 'idhi' as 'it'. You can refer to both of them as 'it'. The only concept here is when you use 'adhi', it means that you are referring to something which is far away and when you use 'idhi', then it means that you are referring to something which is nearby, similar to 'that and this' in English. But whether you are able to figure out something which is far away or nearby doesn't matter, you should simply take a random guess and use 'adhi or idhi'.

2) The verb suffix for miiru (you), aayana (he), aavida (she) and vaaLLu (they) is '-ru'.

a) You don't have to worry or get confused on how to recognize the difference when all of them have the same suffix; that's why I have mentioned that you should use the pronoun mandatorily while conjugating a verb. This will help you to distinguish between them. The reason why we use the suffix '-ru' for all these four pronouns is because the suffix '-ru' refers to politeness; that's why we use the same suffix for you/he/she/they (formal/polite).

b) In Telugu, whenever you refer to a group of people, then you will always be polite e.g., 'they'. Since you would never know who will be included in this group of people, it's always better to be polite than being disrespectful to that person. That's why we use the suffix '-ru' for the pronoun 'vaaLLu' (they) as well.

c) Actually, this makes your life much easier. Whenever you refer to a person or a group of people with whom you want to be polite to, simply conjugate the verb using the verb suffix '-ru'.

3) The verb suffix for manamu (we) (incl), meemu (we) (excl) is 'mu'. The distinction between whether you have included the listener or not included the listener will be conveyed through the pronoun, so you don't have to worry about that. Simply use the same suffix for both the forms of 'we'.

4) Because of the above-mentioned reasons, earlier I wrote that it is mandatory that you should always mention the pronoun when you conjugate a verb so that it is clear and easy for the listener to figure out whom or what are you referring to.

Example: The below table shows the verb conjugation of 'thinu' (to eat) in Present continuous (PC) tense.

Pronoun	Verb root	PC Tense Suffix	Verb Suffix	PC Tense	English Translation
nenu	thinu	-tunnaa-	-nu	thintunnaanu	I am eating
nuvvu	thinu	-tunnaa-	-vu	thintunnaavu	You are eating (impolite)
miiru	thinu	-tunnaa-	-ru	thintunnaaru	You are eating (formal/polite)
aayana	thinu	-tunnaa-		thintunnaaru	He is eating (formal/polite)
aavida	thinu	-tunnaa-		thintunnaaru	She is eating (formal/polite)
vaaLLu	thinu	-tunnaa-		thintunnaaru	They are eating
athanu	thinu	-tunnaa-	-du	thintunnaadu	He is eating (impolite)
meemu	thinu	-tunnaa-	-mu	thintunnaamu	we are eating (listener Inclusive)
manamu	thinu	-tunnaa-	-mu	thintunnaamu	we are eating (listener Exclusive)
aame/ adhi/idhi	thinu	-	thundhi	thintundhi	She/that/this is eating (impolite)
avi/ivi	thinu	-tunnaa-	-yi	thintunnaayi	Those/These are eating

Example: The below table shows the verb conjugation of 'thinu' (to eat) in Future tense.

Pronoun	Verb root	Future Tense Suffix	Verb Suffix	Suffix combination with verb root	Future Tense	English Translation
nenu	thinu	-taa-	-nu	thinu+taa+nu	thintaanu	I will eat
nuvvu	thinu	-taa-	-vu	thinu+taa+vu	thintaavu	You will eat (impolite)
miiru	thinu	-taa-	-ru	thinu+taa+ru	thintaaru	You will eat (formal/polite)
aayana	thinu	-taa-		thinu+taa+ru	thintaaru	He will eat (formal/polite)
aavida	thinu	-taa-		thinu+taa+ru	thintaaru	She will eat (formal/polite)
vaaLLu	thinu	-taa-		thinu+taa+ru	thintaaru	They will eat
athanu	thinu	-taa-	-du	thinu+taa+du	thintaadu	He will eat (impolite)
meemu	thinu	-taa-	-mu	thinu+taa+mu	thintaamu	we will eat (inclusive)
manamu	thinu	-taa-	-mu	thinu+taa+mu	thintaamu	we will eat (exclusive)
aame/ adhi/idhi	thinu	-	thundhi	thintundhi	thintundhi	She/that/this will eat (impolite)
avi/ivi	thinu	-taa-	-yi	thinu+taa+yi	thintaayi	Those/These will eat

Note: In the above verb conjugation for the pronouns 'aame/adhi/idhi', I have mentioned 'thintundhi' instead of 'thinthundhi'. This is an exceptional case, please learn it as it is.

Note: As mentioned earlier, In Telugu, the verb conjugation for Present tense and Future tense will always be the same. The sentence below will make it clearer to you.

Telugu Sentence	English Meaning
nenu thinnaanu (Past tense)	I ate
nenu repu thintaanu (Future tense)	**I will eat tomorrow**
nenu ivvala thintaanu (Present tense)	**I eat today**
nenu thintunnaanu	I am eating
meemu ninna thinnaamu	We ate yesterday
meemu ivvala thintaamu	**We eat today**
meemu repu thintaamu	**We will eat tomorrow**
nuvvu ninna thinnavu	You ate yesterday
nuvvu ivvala thintaavu	**You eat today**
nuvvu repu thintaavu	**You will eat tomorrow**

As you can see in the above table, I have highlighted the Future and Present tense conjugated sentence and they both share the same format e.g., "thintaanu (Future) / thintaanu (Present)". This how we conjugate sentences in Telugu.

Exercises:

A) Translate the following sentences into Telugu.

(Some translation to help you out with this exercise: Yesterday = ninna, Today = i roju, Tomorrow = repu, Lunch or Dinner = bhojanam, Sound = shabdham, now = ippudu, ice cream= ice cream)

1. They are eating lunch now.

2. She ate ice cream today (Polite)

3. We ate ice cream yesterday.

4. You will eat ice cream. (Polite)

5. He eats ice cream. (Impolite)

6. She is eating ice cream (Impolite)

7. These are eating ice cream.

Most Important verb 'undhu' 'to be'

The three words given in the table below comes from the root verb 'undhu' (to be), and it indicates neutral (animals, things, etc.). Since these three words are important and we use them a lot in Telugu, you should memorize these three words.

The below table represents the singular form of the verb 'undhu'.

Neuter form of 'undhu'	Meaning in English
undeedhi	It was
undhi	It is
untundhi	It will be

The below table represents the plural form of the verb 'undhu'.

Neuter form of 'undhu'	Meaning in English
unnaayi	those were
untaayi	those are
undeevi	those will be

Note: The word 'undhu' is an important and frequently used word in Telugu. The word 'undhi' alone also gives you the meaning of 'Have' or 'it is there' or 'are there' etc., it is a multipurpose word and it is used in many sentence formations in Telugu.

Example:

a) naadheggara okka pen undhi.

lit: with me a pen have.

t: I have a pen with me.

b) akkada okka pen undhi.

lit: there a pen is.

t: there is a pen.

Forms of 'undhu'	Multiple meanings in English
undeedhi (singular) / undeevi (plural)	Had
	Was available
	It was there
	Was there
	There was
undhi (singular) / unnaayi (plural)	Have
	Is available
	It is there, available
	Are there
	There are
	Is there
	There is
untundhi (singular) / untaayi (plural)	Will have
	Will be available
	It will be there
	Will be there
	There will be

Example:

c) Taxi Factorylo undhi

lit: taxi in the factor is

t: taxi is in the factory

d) Taxi Factorylo untundhi

lit: taxi in the factor will be

t: taxi will be in the factory

Note: Here 'Taxi' represents 'It' 'adhi'

e) Taxi Factorylo undeedhi

lit: taxi in the factor was

t: taxi was in the factory

f) yenni pusthakaalu unnaayi?

t/lit: how many books are there?

g) aidhu pusthakaalu unnaayi

lit: five books there are

t: there are five books.

h) tomatoes unnaayi

t/lit: tomatoes are available

i) tomatoes unnaayaa?

t: is tomato available?

j) tomato undhi

t/lit: tomato is available

k) tomato undhaa?

t: is tomato available?

l) yenni tomatoes unnaayi?

t/lit: how many tomatoes are there?

Verb Classes:

I have classified some important verbs into 8 different classes based on a pattern of their verb root endings and verb conjugation, but this is not concrete. They are applicable for most of the verb roots with the same pattern but there are few exceptions as well.

Verb	Translation	Verb	Translation	Verb	Translation
Class 1					
cheyyi	To do / make	veyyi	To drop	koyyi	To cut
muyyi	To close	raayi	To write	chuudu	To see / look
giyyi	To draw				
Class 2					
nilabadu	To stand	padu	To fall	kanapadu	To able to see
Class 3					
thinu	To eat	vinu	To hear	konu	To buy
Class 4					
thippu	To turn something	thirugu	To ask a person to turn	nimpu	To fill
kalupu	To mix	dhigu	To get down	pampu	To send
Class 5					
piluvu	To call	ivvu	To give	chupinchu	To show
naduvu	To walk	aruvu	To shout	vochcha	To come
Class 6					
kaluvu	To meet	chadhuvu	To read	perugu	To grow
adugu	To ask				
Class 7					
pettu	To keep/ put	kottu	To hit	thittu	To scold
kattu	To build				
Class 8					
aaduko	To play	paduko	To lie down	nerchuko	To learn

Class 1 verbs

In class 1 verbs, you will replace the ending of the verb root 'yi' with 's' while conjugating the verb in past, present continuous, and future tense.

Example: Class 1 root verb "raayi" (to write)

nenu (raayi + -aa + -nu) = nenu raasaanu (I wrote)

In the above example you can see that I automatically changed the verb root ending from 'yi' to 's'. You may ask me "why do we do this?" Let me give you a simple explanation.

Try conjugating the same without changing the verb root ending and pronounce them.

Example: nenu (raayi + -aa + -nu) = nenu raayiaanu (I wrote) (Incorrect)

I am sure that you will struggle and a portion of your throat will even hurt a little while you do. So, that's why those who designed the Telugu language changed the ending while conjugating the verb so that it's easy for you to pronounce and the pronunciation becomes synchronized and sounds better as well.

Note: This also works as an indicator for you, whenever you pronounce a word or a sentence in Telugu and it's difficult for you to pronounce and a portion of your throat hurts as well, then it means that you are not pronouncing it properly and you are making a mistake.

1) raayi (to write)

Pronoun	Past	Continuous	Future
nenu (I)	raa**saa**nu	raa**sthunnaa**nu	raa**sthaa**nu
nuvvu (You) (impolite)	raa**saa**vu	raa**sthunnaa**vu	raa**sthaa**vu
miiru (You) (Polite)	raa**saa**ru	raa**sthunnaa**ru	raa**sthaa**ru
aayana (He) (polite)			
aavida (She) (polite)			
vaaLLu (They)			
athanu (He) (impolite)	raa**saa**du	raa**sthunaa**du	raa**sthaa**du
meemu (We) (inclusive)	raa**saa**mu	raa**sthunaa**mu	raa**sthaa**mu
manamu (We) (exclusive)	raa**saa**mu	raa**sthunaa**mu	raa**sthaa**mu
aame/adhi/idhi	raa**sindhi**	raa**sthundhi**	raa**sthundhi**
avi/ivi (Those/These)	raa**saa**yi	raa**sthunnaa**yi	raa**sthaa**yi

The suffix for Past tense = '-aa', Present Continuous = '-thunnaa', Future tense = '-thaa'.

As mentioned earlier, this tense suffix is fixed most of the time, there are very few exceptions where we change the tense suffix.

2) cheyyi (to do, to make)

Pronoun	Past	Translation	Present Continuous	Translation
nenu (I)	chesaanu	I did	chesthunnaanu	I am doing
nuvvu (You) (imp)	chesaavu	You did	chesthunnaavu	You are doing
miiru (You) (polite)	chesaaru	You did	chesthunnaaru	You are doing
aayana (He) (polite)		He did		He is doing
aavida (She) (polite)		She did		She is doing
vaaLLu (They)		They did		They are doing
athanu (He) (impolite)	chesaadu	He did	chesthunaadu	He is doing
meemu (We) (incl)	chesaamu	We did	chesthunaamu	We are doing
manamu (We) (excl)	chesaamu	We did	chesthunaamu	We are doing
aame/adhi/idhi	chesindhi	She, that, this did	chesthundhi	She/that/this is doing
avi/ivi (Those/These)	chesaayi	These, those did	chesthunnaayi	Those/These are doing

Pronoun	Future	Translation
nenu (I)	chesthaanu	I will do
nuvvu (You) (impolite)	chesthaavu	You will do
miiru (You) (polite)	chesthaaru	You will do
aayana (He) (polite)		He will do
aavida (She) (polite)		She will do
vaaLLu (They)		They will do
athanu (He) (impolite)	chesthaadu	He will do
meemu (We) (inclusive)	chesthaamu	We will do
manamu (We) (exclusive)	chesthaamu	We will do
aame/adhi/idhi	chesthundhi	She/that/this will do
avi/ivi (Those/These)	chesthaayi	Those/These will do

3) veyyi (to drop something): As mentioned before here the 'yi' will be replaced by 's' while conjugating the verb.

Pronoun	Past	Present Continuous	Future
nenu (I)	ves + aa + nu vesaanu	ves + thunnaa + nu vesthunnaanu	ves + thaa + nu vestaanu
nuvvu (You) (impolite)	ves + aa + vu vesaavu	ves + thunnaa + vu vesthunnaavu	ves + thaa + vu vesthaavu
miiru (You) (polite) aayana (He) (polite) aavida (She) (polite) vaaLLu (They)	ves + aa + ru vesaaru	ves + thunnaa + ru vesthunnaaru	ves + thaa + ru vesthaaru
athanu (He) (impolite)	ves + aa + du vesaadu	ves + thunnaa + du vesthunaadu	ves + thaa + du vesthaadu
meemu (We) (inclusive)	ves + aa + mu vesaamu	ves + thunnaa + mu vesthunaamu	ves + thaa + mu vesthaamu
manamu (We) (exclusive)	ves + aa + mu vesaamu	ves + thunnaa + mu vesthunaamu	ves + thaa + mu vesthaamu
aame/adhi/idhi	**vesindhi**	**vesthundhi**	**vesthundhi**
avi/ivi (Those/These)	ves + aa + yi vesaayi	ves + thunnaa + yi vesthunnaayi	ves + thaa + yi vesthaayi

4) muyyi (to close): the 'yi' will be replaced by 's' while conjugating the verb.

Pronoun	Past	Translation
nenu (I)	**mus + aa + nu** musaanu	I closed
nuvvu (You) (impolite)	**mus + aa + vu** musaavu	You closed
miiru (You) (polite)		You closed
aayana (He) (polite)	**mus + aa + ru** musaaru	He closed
aavida (She) (polite)		She closed
vaaLLu (They)		They closed
athanu (He) (impolite)	**mus + aa + du** musaadu	He closed
meemu (We) (inclusive)	**mus + aa + mu** musaamu	We closed
manamu (We) (exclusive)	**mus + aa + mu** musaamu	We closed
aame/adhi/idhi	**musindhi**	She, that, this closed
avi/ivi (Those/These)	**mus + aa + yi** musaayi	These, those closed

Exercises:

b) Conjugate the following

1a. Verb: muyyi (to close) (Present continuous)

Example: I am closing = nenu musthunnaanu

I am closing	=	
You are closing (impolite)	=	
You are closing (polite)	=	
He is closing (polite)	=	
She is closing (polite)	=	
They are closing	=	
We are closing (incl/excl)	=	
She/that/this is closing (impolite)	=	
Those/These are closing	=	

1b. Verb: muyyi (to close) (Future)

Example: I will close = nenu musthaanu

I will close	=	
You will close (impolite)	=	
You will close (polite)	=	
He will close (polite)	=	
She will close (polite)	=	
They will close	=	
We will close (incl/excl)	=	
She/that/this will close (impolite)	=	
Those/These will close	=	

5) koyyi (to cut)

Pronoun	Past	Translation	Present Continuous	Translation
nenu (I)	kosaanu	I cut	kosthunnaanu	I am cutting
nuvvu (You) (imp)	kosaavu	You cut	kosthunnaavu	You are cutting
miiru (You) (polite)	kosaaru	You cut	kosthunnaaru	You are cutting
aayana (He) (polite)		He cut		He is cutting
aavida (She) (polite)		She cut		She is cutting
vaaLLu (They)		They cut		They are cutting
athanu (He) (impolite)	kosaadu	He cut	kosthunaadu	He is cutting
meemu (We) (incl)	kosaamu	We cut	kosthunaamu	We are cutting
manamu (We) (excl)	kosaamu	We cut	kosthunaamu	We are cutting
aame/adhi/idhi	kosindhi	She, that, this cut	kosthundhi	She/that/this is cutting
avi/ivi (Those/These)	kosaayi	These, those cut	kosthunnaayi	Those/These are cutting

Pronoun	Future	Translation
nenu (I)	kosthaanu	I will cut
nuvvu (You) (impolite)	kosthaavu	You will cut
miiru (You) (polite)	kosthaaru	You will cut
aayana (He) (polite)		He will cut
aavida (She) (polite)		She will cut
vaaLLu (They)		They will cut
athanu (He) (impolite)	kosthaadu	He will cut
meemu (We) (inclusive)	kosthaamu	We will cut
manamu (We) (exclusive)	kosthaamu	We will cut
aame/adhi/idhi	kosthundhi	She/that/this will cut
avi/ivi (Those/These)	kosthaayi	Those/These will cut

6) giyyi (to draw)

Pronoun	Past	Translation	Present Continuous	Translation
nenu (I)	gisaanu	I drew	gisthunnaanu	I am drawing
nuvvu (You) (imp)	gisaavu	You drew	gisthunnaavu	You are drawing
miiru (You) (polite)	gisaaru	You drew	gisthunnaaru	You are drawing
aayana (He) (polite)		He drew		He is drawing
aavida (She) (polite)		She drew		She is drawing
vaaLLu (They)		They drew		They are drawing
athanu (He) (impolite)	gisaadu	He drew	gisthunaadu	He is drawing
meemu (We) (incl)	gisaamu	We drew	gisthunaamu	We are drawing
manamu (We) (excl)	gisaamu	We drew	gisthunaamu	We are drawing
aame/adhi/idhi	gisindhi	She, that, this drew	gisthundhi	She/that/this is drawing
avi/ivi (Those/These)	gisaayi	These, those drew	gisthunnaayi	Those/These are drawing

Pronoun	Future	Translation
nenu (I)	gisthaanu	I will draw
nuvvu (You) (impolite)	gisthaavu	You will draw
miiru (You) (polite)	gisthaaru	You will draw
aayana (He) (polite)		He will draw
aavida (She) (polite)		She will draw
vaaLLu (They)		They will draw
athanu (He) (impolite)	gisthaadu	He will draw
meemu (We) (inclusive)	gisthaamu	We will draw
manamu (We) (exclusive)	gisthaamu	We will draw
aame/adhi/idhi	gisthundhi	She/that/this will draw
avi/ivi (Those/These)	gisthaayi	Those/These will draw

7) chudu (to see)

Pronoun	Past	Translation	Present Continuous	Translation
nenu (I)	chusaanu	I saw	chusthunnaanu	I am seeing
nuvvu (You) (imp)	chusaavu	You saw	chusthunnaavu	You are seeing
miiru (You) (polite)	chusaaru	You saw	chusthunnaaru	You are seeing
aayana (He) (polite)		He saw		He is seeing
aavida (She) (polite)		She saw		She is seeing
vaaLLu (They)		They saw		They are seeing
athanu (He) (impolite)	chusaadu	He saw	chusthunaadu	He is seeing
meemu (We) (incl)	chusaamu	We saw	chusthunaamu	We are seeing
manamu (We) (excl)	chusaamu	We saw	chusthunaamu	We are seeing
aame/adhi/idhi	chusindhi	She, that, this saw	chusthundhi	She/that/this is seeing
avi/ivi (Those/These)	chusaayi	These, those saw	chusthunnaayi	Those/These are seeing

Pronoun	Future	Translation
nenu (I)	chusthaanu	I will see
nuvvu (You) (impolite)	chusthaavu	You will see
miiru (You) (polite)	chusthaaru	You will see
aayana (He) (polite)		He will see
aavida (She) (polite)		She will see
vaaLLu (They)		They will see
athanu (He) (impolite)	chusthaadu	He will see
meemu (We) (inclusive)	chusthaamu	We will see
manamu (We) (exclusive)	chusthaamu	We will see
aame/adhi/idhi	chusthundhi	She/that/this will see
avi/ivi (Those/These)	chusthaayi	Those/These will see

Class 2 verbs

In class 2 verbs, you will add an additional 'd' to the verb root while conjugating the verb in the past. But when you conjugate the verb in the present continuous and future tense, then you will not add anything to the verb root.

Example: Class 2 root verb "nilabadu" (to stand)

nenu (nilabadu + -d + -aa + -nu) = nenu nilabaddaanu (I stood)

nenu (nilabadu + -thaa + -nu) = nenu nilabaduthaanu (I will stand)

8) nilabadu (to stand)

Pronoun	Past	Continuous	Future
nenu (I)	nilabadd**aa**nu	nilabadu**thunnaa**nu	nilabadu**thaa**nu
nuvvu (You) (impolite)	nilabadd**aa**vu	nilabadu**thunnaa**vu	nilabadu**thaa**vu
miiru (You) (polite)			
aayana (He) (polite)			
aavida (She) (polite)	nilabadd**aa**ru	nilabadu**thunnaa**ru	nilabadu**thaa**ru
vaaLLu (They)			
athanu (He) (impolite)	nilabadd**aa**du	nilabadu**thunaa**du	nilabadu**thaa**du
meemu (We) (inclusive)	nilabadd**aa**mu	nilabadu**thunaa**mu	nilabadu**thaa**mu
manamu (We) (exclusive)	nilabadd**aa**mu	nilabadu**thunaa**mu	nilabadu**thaa**mu
aame/adhi/idhi	nilabadindhi	nilabaduthundhi	nilabaduthundhi
avi/ivi (Those/These)	nilabadd**aa**yi	nilabadu**thunnaa**yi	nilabadu**thaa**yi

9) padu (to fall, lie down)

Pronoun	Past	Translation	Present Continuous	Translation
nenu (I)	paddaanu	I fell	paduthunnaanu	I am falling
nuvvu (You) (imp)	paddaavu	You fell	paduthunnavu	You are falling
miiru (You) (polite)	paddaaru	You fell	paduthunnaru	You are falling
aayana (He) (polite)		He fell		He is falling
aavida (She) (polite)		She fell		She is falling
vaaLLu (They)		They fell		They are falling
athanu (He) (impolite)	paddaadu	He fell	paduthunnadu	He is falling
meemu (We) (incl)	paddaamu	We fell	paduthunnaamu	We are falling
manamu (We) (excl)	paddaamu	We fell	paduthunnaamu	We are falling
aame/adhi/idhi	padindi	She, that, this fell	paduthundhi	She/that/this is falling
avi/ivi (Those/These)	padaayi	These, those fell	paduthunnaayi	Those/These are falling

Pronoun	Future	Translation
nenu (I)	paduthaanu	I will fall
nuvvu (You) (impolite)	paduthaavu	You will fall
miiru (You) (polite)	paduthaaru	You will fall
aayana (He) (polite)		He will fall
aavida (She) (polite)		She will fall
vaaLLu (They)		They will fall
athanu (He) (impolite)	paduthaadu	He will fall
meemu (We) (inclusive)	paduthaamu	We will fall
manamu (We) (exclusive)	paduthaamu	We will fall
aame/adhi/idhi	paduthundhi	She/that/this will fall
avi/ivi (Those/These)	paduthaayi	Those/These will fall

10) kanapadu (to be able to see):

Pronoun	Past	Translation
nenu (I)	**kanapadd + aa + nu** kanapaddaanu	I was able to see
nuvvu (You) (impolite)	**kanapadd + aa + vu** kanapaddaavu	You were able to see
miiru (You) (polite)	**kanapadd + aa + ru** kanapaddaaru	You were able to see
aayana (He) (polite)		He was able to see
aavida (She) (polite)		She was able to see
vaaLLu (They)		They were able to see
athanu (He) (impolite)	**kanapadd + aa + du** kanapaddaadu	He was able to see
meemu (We) (inclusive)	**kanapadd + aa + mu** kanapaddaamu	We were able to see
manamu (We) (exclusive)	**kanapadd + aa + mu** kanapaddaamu	We were able to see
aame/adhi/idhi	**kanapadindhi**	She, that, this was able to see
avi/ivi (Those/These)	**kanapadd + aa + yi** kanapaddaayi	These, those were able to see

Conjugate the following

2a. Verb: kanapadu (to be able to see) (Present continuous)

Example: I am able to see = nenu kanapaduthunnaanu

I am able to see	=	
You are able to see (informal/impolite)	=	
You are able to see (formal/polite)	=	
He is able to see (formal/polite)	=	
She is able to see (polite)	=	
They are able to see	=	
We are able to see (incl/excl)	=	
She/that/this is able to see (impolite)	=	
Those/These are able to see	=	

2b. Verb: kanapadu (to be able to see) (Future)

I will be able to see	=	
You will be able to see (informal/impolite)	=	
You will be able to see (formal/polite)	=	
He will be able to see (formal/polite)	=	
She will be able to see (polite)	=	
They will be able to see	=	
We will be able to see (incl/excl)	=	
She/that/this will be able to see (impolite)	=	
Those/These will be able to see	=	

Class 3 verbs

In class 3 verbs, you will add another 'n' to the verb root while conjugating the verb in the past. But when you conjugate the verb in the present continuous and future tense, then you will not add anything to the verb root.

Example: Class 3 root verb "vinu" (to hear)

nenu (vinu + -n + -aa + -nu) = nenu vinnaaanu (I heard)

nenu (vinu + -taa + -nu) = nenu vintaanu (I will hear)

11) vinu (to hear)

Pronoun	Past	Continuous	Future
nenu (I)	vinnu + aa + nu (vinnaanu)	vinu + tunnaa + nu (vintunnaanu)	vinu + taa + nu (vintaanu)
nuvvu (You) (impolite)	vinu + aa + vu (vinnaavu)	vinu + tunnaa + vu (vintunnaavu)	vinu + taa + vu (vintaavu)
miiru (You) (polite) aayana (He) (polite) aavida (She) (polite) vaaLLu (They)	vinu + aa + ru (vinnaaru)	vinu + tunnaa + ru (vintunnaaru)	vinu + taa + ru (vintaaru)
athanu (He) (impolite)	vinu + aa + du (vinnaadu)	vinu + tunnaa + du (vintunnaadu)	vinu + taa + du (vintaadu)
meemu (We) (incl)	vinu + aa + mu (vinnaamu)	vinu + tunnaa + mu (vintunnaamu)	vinu + taa + mu (vintaamu)
manamu (We) (excl)	vinu + aa + mu (vinnaamu)	vinu + tunnaa + mu (vintunnaamu)	vinu + taa + mu (vintaamu)
aame/adhi/idhi	vinnadhi	vintundhi	vintundhi
avi/ivi (Those/These)	vinnaayi	vintaayi	vintunnaayi

12) konu (to buy)

Pronoun	Past	Translation	Present Continuous	Translation
nenu (I)	konnaanu	I bought	kontunnaanu	I am buying
nuvvu (You) (imp)	konnaavu	You bought	kontunnaavu	You are buying
miiru (You) (polite)	konnaaru	You bought	kontunnaaru	You are buying
aayana (He) (polite)		He bought		He is buying
aavida (She) (polite)		She bought		She is buying
vaaLLu (They)		They bought		They are buying
athanu (He) (impolite)	konnaadu	He bought	kontunnaadu	He is buying
meemu (We) (incl)	konnaamu	We bought	kontunnaamu	We are buying
manamu (We) (excl)	konnaamu	We bought	kontunnaamu	We are buying
aame/adhi/idhi	konnadhi	She, that, this bought	kontundhi	She/that/this is buying
avi/ivi (Those/These)	konnaayi	These, those bought	kontunnaayi	Those/These are buying

Pronoun	Future	Translation
nenu (I)	kontaanu	I will buy
nuvvu (You) (impolite)	kontaavu	You will buy
miiru (You) (polite)	kontaaru	You will buy
aayana (He) (polite)		He will buy
aavida (She) (polite)		She will buy
vaaLLu (They)		They will buy
athanu (He) (impolite)	kontaadu	He will buy
meemu (We) (inclusive)	kontaamu	We will buy
manamu (We) (exclusive)	kontaamu	We will buy
aame/adhi/idhi	kontundhi	She/that/this will buy
avi/ivi (Those/These)	kontaayi	Those/These will buy

Class 4 verbs: 13) thippu (to turn something): This verb is mainly used when you turn an object and parts of a body.

Pronoun	Past	Translation	PC	Translation
nenu (I)	thippaanu	I turned	thipputhunaanu	I am turning
nuvvu (You) (imp)	thippaavu	You turned	thipputhunaavu	You are turning
miiru (You) (polite)	thippaaru	You turned	thipputhunaaru	You are turning
aayana (He) (polite)		He turned		He is turning
aavida (She) (polite)		She turned		She is turning
vaaLLu (They)		They turned		They are turning
athanu (He) (impolite)	thippaadu	He turned	thipputhunnaadu	He is turning
meemu (We) (incl)	thippaamu	We turned	thipputhunaamu	We are turning
manamu (We) (excl)	thippaamu	We turned	thipputhunaamu	We are turning
aame/adhi/idhi	thippindhi	She, that, this turned	thipputhundhi	She/that/this is turning
avi/ivi (Those/These)	thippaayi	These, those turned	thipputhunnaayi	Those/These are turning

Pronoun	Future	Translation
nenu (I)	thipputhaanu	I will turn
nuvvu (You) (impolite)	thipputhaavu	You will turn
miiru (You) (polite)	thipputhaaru	You will turn
aayana (He) (polite)		He will turn
aavida (She) (polite)		She will turn
vaaLLu (They)		They will turn
athanu (He) (impolite)	thipputhaadu	He will turn
meemu (We) (inclusive)	thipputhaamu	We will turn
manamu (We) (exclusive)	thipputhaamu	We will turn
aame/adhi/idhi	thipputhundhi	She/that/this will turn
avi/ivi (Those/These)	thipputhaayi	Those/These will turn

14) thirugu (to turn someone), This verb is mainly used when you turn a person or request to turn a person. So, with this verb we should always have an object to make a sentence.

Pronoun	Past	Translation	PC	Translation
nenu (I)	thirigaanu	I turned	thiruguthunaanu	I am turning
nuvvu (You) (imp)	thirigaavu	You turned	thiruguthunaavu	You are turning
miiru (You) (polite)	thirigaaru	You turned	thiruguthunaaru	You are turning
aayana (He) (polite)		He turned		He is turning
aavida (She) (polite)		She turned		She is turning
vaaLLu (They)		They turned		They are turning
athanu (He) (impolite)	thirigaadu	He turned	thiruguthunnaadu	He is turning
meemu (We) (incl)	thirigaamu	We turned	thiruguthunaamu	We are turning
manamu (We) (excl)	thirigaamu	We turned	thiruguthunaamu	We are turning
aame/adhi/idhi	thirigindhi	She, that, this turned	thiruguthundhi	She/that/this is turning
avi/ivi (Those/These)	thirigaayi	These, those turned	thiruguthunnaayi	Those/These are turning

Pronoun	Future	Translation
nenu (I)	thiruguthaanu	I will turn
nuvvu (You) (impolite)	thiruguthaavu	You will turn
miiru (You) (polite)	thiruguthaaru	You will turn
aayana (He) (polite)		He will turn
aavida (She) (polite)		She will turn
vaaLLu (They)		They will turn
athanu (He) (impolite)	thiruguthaadu	He will turn
meemu (We) (inclusive)	thiruguthaamu	We will turn
manamu (We) (exclusive)	thiruguthaamu	We will turn
aame/adhi/idhi	thiruguthundhi	She/that/this will turn
avi/ivi (Those/These)	thiruguthaayi	Those/These will turn

15) kalupu (to mix)

Pronoun	Past	Translation	Present Continuous	Translation
nenu (I)	kalipaanu	I mixed	kaluputhunaanu	I am mixing
nuvvu (You) (imp)	kalipaavu	You mixed	kaluputhunaavu	You are mixing
miiru (You) (polite)	kalipaaru	You mixed	kaluputhunaaru	You are mixing
aayana (He) (polite)		He mixed		He is mixing
aavida (She) (polite)		She mixed		She is mixing
vaaLLu (They)		They mixed		They are mixing
athanu (He) (impolite)	kalipaadu	He mixed	kaluputhunnaadu	He is mixing
meemu (We) (incl)	kalipaamu	We mixed	kaluputhunaamu	We are mixing
manamu (We) (excl)	kalipaamu	We mixed	kaluputhunaamu	We are mixing
aame/adhi/idhi	kalipindhi	She, that, this mixed	kaluputhundhi	She/that/this is mixing
avi/ivi (Those/These)	kalipaayi	These, those mixed	kaluputhunnaayi	Those/These are mixing

Pronoun	Future	Translation
nenu (I)	kaluputhaanu	I will mix
nuvvu (You) (impolite)	kaluputhaavu	You will mix
miiru (You) (polite)	kaluputhaaru	You will mix
aayana (He) (polite)		He will mix
aavida (She) (polite)		She will mix
vaaLLu (They)		They will mix
athanu (He) (impolite)	kaluputhaadu	He will mix
meemu (We) (inclusive)	kaluputhaamu	We will mix
manamu (We) (exclusive)	kaluputhaamu	We will mix
aame/adhi/idhi	kaluputhundhi	She/that/this will mix
avi/ivi (Those/These)	kaluputhaayi	Those/These will mix

16) dhigu (to get down)

Pronoun	Past	Translation	PC	Translation
nenu (I)	dhigaanu	I got down	dhiguthunaanu	I am getting down
nuvvu (You) (imp)	dhigaavu	You got down	dhiguthunaavu	You are getting down
miiru (You) (polite)	dhigaaru	You got down	dhiguthunaaru	You are getting down
aayana (He) (polite)		He got down		He is getting down
aavida (She) (polite)		She got down		She is getting down
vaaLLu (They)		They got down		They are getting down
athanu (He)	dhigaadu	He got down	dhiguthunnaadu	He is getting down
meemu (We) (incl)	dhigaamu	We got down	dhiguthunaamu	We are getting down
manamu (We) (excl)	dhigaamu	We got down	dhiguthunaamu	We are getting down
aame/adhi/idhi	dhigindhi	She, that, this got down	dhiguthundhi	She/that/this is getting down
avi/ivi (Those/These)	dhigaayi	These, those got down	dhiguthunnaayi	Those/These are getting down

Pronoun	Future	Translation
nenu (I)	dhiguthaanu	I will get down
nuvvu (You) (impolite)	dhiguthaavu	You will get down
miiru (You) (polite)	dhiguthaaru	You will get down
aayana (He) (polite)		He will get down
aavida (She) (polite)		She will get down
vaaLLu (They)		They will get down
athanu (He) (impolite)	dhiguthaadu	He will get down
meemu (We) (inclusive)	dhiguthaamu	We will get down
manamu (We) (exclusive)	dhiguthaamu	We will get down
aame/adhi/idhi	dhiguthundhi	She/that/this will get down
avi/ivi (Those/These)	dhiguthaayi	Those/These will get down

Conjugate the following

17) nimpu (to fill)

3a. Verb: nimpu (to fill) (Past tense)

Example: I filled = nenu nimppaanu

I filled	=	
You filled (informal/impolite)	=	
You filled (polite)	=	
He filled (polite)	=	
She filled (polite)	=	
They filled	=	
We filled (incl/excl)	=	
She/that/this filled (impolite)	=	
Those/These filled	=	

3b. Verb: nimpu (to fill) (Present continuous)

Example: I am filling = nenu nimputhunnaanu

I am filling	=	
You are filling (informal/impolite)	=	
You are filling (polite)	=	
He is filling (polite)	=	
She is filling (polite)	=	
They are filling	=	
We are filling (incl/excl)	=	
She/that/this is filling (impolite)	=	
Those/These are filling	=	

3c. Verb: nimpu (to fill) (Future tense)

Example: I will fill = nenu nimpputhaanu

I will fill	=	
You will fill (informal/impolite)	=	
You will fill (polite)	=	
He will fill (polite)	=	
She will fill (polite)	=	
They will fill	=	
We will fill (incl/excl)	=	
She/that/this will fill (impolite)	=	
Those/These will fill	=	

18) pampu (to send)

4a. Verb: pampu (to send) (Past tense)

Example: I sent = nenu pamppaanu

I sent	=	
You sent (informal/impolite)	=	
You sent (polite)	=	
He sent (polite)	=	
She sent (polite)	=	
They sent	=	
We sent (incl/excl)	=	
She/that/this sent (impolite)	=	
Those/These sent	=	

4b. Verb: pampu (to send) (Present continuous)

Example: I am sending = nenu pampputhunnaanu

I am sending	=	
You are sending (informal/impolite)	=	
You are sending (polite)	=	
He is sending (polite)	=	
She is sending (formal)	=	
They are sending	=	
We are sending (incl/excl)	=	
She/that/this is sending (impolite)	=	
Those/These are sending	=	

4c. Verb: pampu (to send) (Future)

Example: I will send = nenu pampputhaanu

I will send	=	
You will send (informal/impolite)	=	
You will send (polite)	=	
He will send (polite)	=	
She will send (formal)	=	
They will send	=	
We will send (incl/excl)	=	
She/that/this will send (impolite)	=	
Those/These will send	=	

Class 5 verbs

19) piluvu (to call)

Pronoun	Past	Translation	PC	Translation
nenu (I)	pilichaanu	I called	pilusthunnaanu	I am calling
nuvvu (You) (imp)	pilichaavu	You called	pilusthunnaavu	You are calling
miiru (You) (polite)	pilichaaru	You called	pilusthunnaaru	You are calling
aayana (He) (polite)		He called		He is calling
aavida (She) (polite)		She called		She is calling
vaaLLu (They)		They called		They are calling
athanu (He) (impolite)	pilichaadu	He called	pilusthunnaadu	He is calling
meemu (We) (incl)	pilichaamu	We called	pilusthunnaamu	We are calling
manamu (We) (excl)	pilichaamu	We called	pilusthunnaamu	We are calling
aame/adhi/idhi	pilichindhi	She, that, this called	pilusthundhi	She/that/this is calling
avi/ivi (Those/These)	pilichaayi	These, those called	pilusthunnaayi	Those/These are calling

Pronoun	Future	Translation
nenu (I)	pilusthaanu	I will call
nuvvu (You) (impolite)	pilusthaavu	You will call
miiru (You) (polite)	pilusthaaru	You will call
aayana (He) (polite)		He will call
aavida (She) (polite)		She will call
vaaLLu (They)		They will call
athanu (He) (impolite)	pilusthaadu	He will call
meemu (We) (inclusive)	pilusthaamu	We will call
manamu (We) (exclusive)	pilusthaamu	We will call
aame/adhi/idhi	pilusthundhi	She/that/this will call
avi/ivi (Those/These)	pilusthaayi	Those/These will call

20) ivvu (to give)

Pronoun	Past	Translation	Present Continuous	Translation
nenu (I)	ichaanu	I gave	isthunnaanu	I am giving
nuvvu (You) (imp)	ichaavu	You gave	isthunnaavu	You are giving
miiru (You) (polite)	ichaaru	You gave	isthunnaaru	You are giving
aayana (He) (polite)		He gave		He is giving
aavida (She) (polite)		She gave		She is giving
vaaLLu (They)		They gave		They are giving
athanu (He) (impolite)	ichaadu	He gave	isthunnaadu	He is giving
meemu (We) (incl)	ichaamu	We gave	isthunnaamu	We are giving
manamu (We) (excl)	ichaamu	We gave	isthunnaamu	We are giving
aame/adhi/idhi	ichindhi	She, that, this gave	isthundhi	She/that/this is giving
avi/ivi (Those/These)	ichaayi	These, those gave	isthunnaayi	Those/These are giving

Pronoun	Future	Translation
nenu (I)	isthaanu	I will give
nuvvu (You) (impolite)	isthaavu	You will give
miiru (You) (polite)	isthaaru	You will give
aayana (He) (polite)		He will give
aavida (She) (polite)		She will give
vaaLLu (They)		They will give
athanu (He) (impolite)	isthaadu	He will give
meemu (We) (inclusive)	isthaamu	We will give
manamu (We) (exclusive)	isthaamu	We will give
aame/adhi/idhi	isthundhi	She/that/this will give
avi/ivi (Those/These)	isthaayi	Those/These will give

21) naduvu (to walk)

Pronoun	Past	Translation	Present Continuous	Translation
nenu (I)	nadichaanu	I walked	nadusthunnaanu	I am walking
nuvvu (You) (imp)	nadichaavu	You walked	nadusthunnaavu	You are walking
miiru (You) (polite)	nadichaaru	You walked	nadusthunnaaru	You are walking
aayana (He) (polite)		He walked		He is walking
aavida (She) (polite)		She walked		She is walking
vaaLLu (They)		They walked		They are walking
athanu (He) (impolite)	nadichaadu	He walked	nadusthunnaadu	He is walking
meemu (We) (incl)	nadichaamu	We walked	nadusthunnaamu	We are walking
manamu (We) (excl)	nadichaamu	We walked	nadusthunnaamu	We are walking
aame/adhi/idhi	nadichindhi	She, that, this walked	nadusthundhi	She/that/this is walking
avi/ivi (Those/These)	nadichaayi	These, those walked	nadusthunnaayi	Those/These are walking

Pronoun	Future	Translation
nenu (I)	nadusthaanu	I will walk
nuvvu (You) (impolite)	nadusthaavu	You will walk
miiru (You) (polite)	nadusthaaru	You will walk
aayana (He) (polite)		He will walk
aavida (She) (polite)		She will walk
vaaLLu (They)		They will walk
athanu (He) (impolite)	nadusthaadu	He will walk
meemu (We) (inclusive)	nadusthaamu	We will walk
manamu (We) (exclusive)	nadusthaamu	We will walk
aame/adhi/idhi	nadusthundhi	She/that/this will walk
avi/ivi (Those/These)	nadusthaayi	Those/These will walk

22) aruvu (to shout)

Pronoun	Past	Translation	Present Continuous	Translation
nenu (I)	arichaanu	I shouted	arusthunnaanu	I am shouting
nuvvu (You) (imp)	arichaavu	You shouted	arusthunnaavu	You are shouting
miiru (You) (polite)	arichaaru	You shouted	arusthunnaaru	You are shouting
aayana (He) (polite)		He shouted		He is shouting
aavida (She) (polite)		She shouted		She is shouting
vaaLLu (They)		They shouted		They are shouting
athanu (He) (impolite)	arichaadu	He shouted	arusthunnaadu	He is shouting
meemu (We) (incl)	arichaamu	We shouted	arusthunnaamu	We are shouting
manamu (We) (excl)	arichaamu	We shouted	arusthunnaamu	We are shouting
aame/adhi/idhi	arichindhi	She, that, this shouted	arusthundhi	She/that/this is shouting
avi/ivi (Those/These)	arichaayi	These, those shouted	arusthunnaayi	Those/These are shouting

Pronoun	Future	Translation
nenu (I)	arusthaanu	I will shout
nuvvu (You) (impolite)	arusthaavu	You will shout
miiru (You) (polite)	arusthaaru	You will shout
aayana (He) (polite)		He will shout
aavida (She) (polite)		She will shout
vaaLLu (They)		They will shout
athanu (He) (impolite)	arusthaadu	He will shout
meemu (We) (inclusive)	arusthaamu	We will shout
manamu (We) (exclusive)	arusthaamu	We will shout
aame/adhi/idhi	arusthundhi	She/that/this will shout
avi/ivi (Those/These)	arusthaayi	Those/These will shout

Conjugate the following

23) chupinchu (to show)

5a. Verb: chupinchu (to show) (Past tense)

Example: I showed = nenu chupinchaanu

I showed	=	
You showed (informal/impolite)	=	
You showed (polite)	=	
He showed (polite)	=	
She showed (polite)	=	
They showed	=	
We showed (incl/excl)	=	
She/that/this showed (impolite)	=	
Those/These showed	=	

5b. Verb: chupinchu (to show) (Present continuous)

Example: I am showing = nenu chupisthunnaanu

I am showing	=	
You are showing (informal/impolite)	=	
You are showing (polite)	=	
He is showing (polite)	=	
She is showing (polite)	=	
They are showing	=	
We are showing (incl/excl)	=	
She/that/this is showing (impolite)	=	
Those/These are showing	=	

5c. Verb: chupinchu (to show) (Future tense)

Example: I will show = nenu chupisthaanu

I will show	=	
You will show (informal/impolite)	=	
You will show (polite)	=	
He will show (polite)	=	
She will show (polite)	=	
They will show	=	
We will show (incl/excl)	=	
She/that/this will show (impolite)	=	
Those/These will show	=	

24) vochcha (to come)

6a. Verb: vochcha (to come) (Past tense)

Example: I came = nenu vochchaanu

I came	=	
You came (informal/impolite)	=	
You came (polite)	=	
He came (polite)	=	
She came (polite)	=	
They came	=	
We came (incl/excl)	=	
She/that/this came (impolite)	=	
Those/These came	=	

6b. Verb: vochcha (to come) (Present continuous)

Example: I am coming = nenu vochchusthunnaanu

I am coming	=	
You are coming (informal/impolite)	=	
You are coming (polite)	=	
He is coming (polite)	=	
She is coming (polite)	=	
They are coming	=	
We are coming (incl/excl)	=	
She/that/this is coming (impolite)	=	
Those/These are coming	=	

6c. Verb: vochcha (to come) (Future)

Example: I will come = nenu vochchusthaanu

I will come	=	
You will come (informal/impolite)	=	
You will come (polite)	=	
He will come (polite)	=	
She will come (polite)	=	
They will come	=	
We will come (incl/excl)	=	
She/that/this will come (impolite)	=	
Those/These will come	=	

Class 6 verbs

25) chadhuvu (to read)

Pronoun	Past	Translation	Present Continuous	Translation
nenu (I)	chadhivaanu	I read	chudhuvuthunnaanu	I am reading
nuvvu (You)	chadhivaavu	You read	chadhuvuthunnaavu	You are reading
miiru (You)	chadhivaaru	You read	chadhuvuthunnaaru	You are reading
aayana (He)		He read		He is reading
aavida (She)		She read		She is reading
vaaLLu (They)		They read		They are reading
athanu (He)	chadhivaadu	He read	chadhuvuthunaadu	He is reading
meemu (We)	chadhivaamu	We read	chadhuvuthunnaamu	We are reading
manamu (We)	chadhivaamu	We read	chadhuvuthunnaamu	We are reading
aame/adhi/idhi	chadhivindhi	She, that, this read	chadhuvuthundhi	She/that/this is reading
avi/ivi	chadhivaayi	These, those read	chadhuvuthunnaayi	Those/These are reading

Pronoun	Future	Translation
nenu (I)	chadhuvuthaanu	I will read
nuvvu (You) (impolite)	chadhuvuthaavu	You will read
miiru (You) (polite)	chadhuvuthaaru	You will read
aayana (He) (polite)		He will read
aavida (She) (polite)		She will read
vaaLLu (They)		They will read
athanu (He) (impolite)	chadhuvuthaadu	He will read
meemu (We) (inclusive)	chadhuvuthaamu	We will read
manamu (We) (exclusive)	chadhuvuthaamu	We will read
aame/adhi/idhi	chadhuvuthundhi	She/that/this will read
avi/ivi (Those/These)	chadhuvuthaayi	Those/These will read

26) kaluvu (to meet)

Pronoun	Past	Translation	PC	Translation
nenu (I)	kalisaanu	I met	kalusuthunnaanu	I am meeting
nuvvu (You) (imp)	kalisaavu	You met	kalusuthunnaavu	You are meeting
miiru (You) (polite)	kalisaaru	You met	kalusuthunnaaru	You are meeting
aayana (He) (polite)		He met		He is meeting
aavida (She) (polite)		She met		She is meeting
vaaLLu (They)		They met		They are meeting
athanu (He) (impolite)	kalisaadu	He met	kalusuthunaadu	He is meeting
meemu (We) (inc)	kalisaamu	We met	kalusuthunnaamu	We are meeting
manamu (We) (excl)	kalisaamu	We met	kalusuthunnaamu	We are meeting
aame/adhi/idhi	kalisindhi	She, that, this met	kalusuthundhi	She/that/this is meeting
avi/ivi (Those/These)	kalisaayi	These, those met	kalusuthunnaayi	Those/These are meeting

Pronoun	Future	Translation
nenu (I)	kalusuthaanu	I will meet
nuvvu (You) (impolite)	kalusuthaavu	You will meet
miiru (You) (polite)	kalusuthaaru	You will meet
aayana (He) (polite)		He will meet
aavida (She) (polite)		She will meet
vaaLLu (They)		They will meet
athanu (He) (impolite)	kalusuthaadu	He will meet
meemu (We) (inclusive)	kalusuthaamu	We will meet
manamu (We) (exclusive)	kalusuthaamu	We will meet
aame/adhi/idhi	kalusuthundhi	She/that/this will meet
avi/ivi (Those/These)	kalusuthaayi	Those/These will meet

27) perugu (to grow)

Pronoun	Past	Translation	Present Continuous	Translation
nenu (I)	perigaanu	I grew	peruguthunnaanu	I am growing
nuvvu (You) (imp)	perigaavu	You grew	peruguthunnaavu	You are growing
miiru (You) (polite)	perigaaru	You grew	peruguthunnaaru	You are growing
aayana (He) (polite)		He grew		He is growing
aavida (She) (polite)		She grew		She is growing
vaaLLu (They)		They grew		They are growing
athanu (He) (impolite)	perigaadu	He grew	peruguthunaadu	He is growing
meemu (We) (incl)	perigaamu	We grew	peruguthunnaamu	We are growing
manamu (We) (excl)	perigaamu	We grew	peruguthunnaamu	We are growing
aame/adhi/idhi	perigindhi	She, that, this grew	peruguthundhi	She/that/this is growing
avi/ivi (Those/These)	perigaayi	These, those grew	peruguthunnaayi	Those/These are growing

Pronoun	Future	Translation
nenu (I)	peruguthaanu	I will grow
nuvvu (You) (impolite)	peruguthaavu	You will grow
miiru (You) (polite)	peruguthaaru	You will grow
aayana (He) (polite)		He will grow
aavida (She) (polite)		She will grow
vaaLLu (They)		They will grow
athanu (He) (impolite)	peruguthaadu	He will grow
meemu (We) (inclusive)	peruguthaamu	We will grow
manamu (We) (exclusive)	peruguthaamu	We will grow
aame/adhi/idhi	peruguthundhi	She/that/this will grow
avi/ivi (Those/These)	peruguthaayi	Those/These will grow

28) adugu (to ask)

Pronoun	Past	Translation	Present Continuous	Translation
nenu (I)	adigaanu	I asked	aduguthunnaanu	I am asking
nuvvu (You) (imp)	adigaavu	You asked	aduguthunnaavu	You are asking
miiru (You) (polite)	adigaaru	You asked	aduguthunnaaru	You are asking
aayana (He) (polite)		He asked		He is asking
aavida (She) (polite)		She asked		She is asking
vaaLLu (They)		They asked		They are asking
athanu (He) (impolite)	adigaadu	He asked	aduguthunaadu	He is asking
meemu (We) (incl)	adigaamu	We asked	aduguthunnaamu	We are asking
manamu (We) (excl)	adigaamu	We asked	aduguthunnaamu	We are asking
aame/adhi/idhi	adigindhi	She, that, this asked	aduguthundhi	She/that/this is asking
avi/ivi (Those/These)	adigaayi	These, those asked	aduguthunnaayi	Those/These are asking

Pronoun	Future	Translation
nenu (I)	aduguthaanu	I will ask
nuvvu (You) (impolite)	aduguthaavu	You will ask
miiru (You) (polite)	aduguthaaru	You will ask
aayana (He) (polite)		He will ask
aavida (She) (polite)		She will ask
vaaLLu (They)		They will ask
athanu (He) (impolite)	aduguthaadu	He will ask
meemu (We) (inclusive)	aduguthaamu	We will ask
manamu (We) (exclusive)	aduguthaamu	We will ask
aame/adhi/idhi	aduguthundhi	She/that/this will ask
avi/ivi (Those/These)	aduguthaayi	Those/These will ask

Class 7 verbs

In class 7 verbs: Past tense conjugation: When you conjugate the verb in the past tense, then you will not change the verb root you will simply use them as it is

Present continuous conjugation: You will replace the letter 'tt' with 'd'.

Future conjugation: You will replace the letter 'ttu' with 'da'

Example: Class 7 root verb "kattu" (to build)

nenu (kattu + -aa + -nu) = nenu kattaanu (I built) (Past)

nenu (kattu + -thunnaa + -nu) = nenu kaduthunnaanu (I am building) (Present continuous)

nenu (kattu + -thaa + -nu) = nenu kadathaanu (I will build) (Future)

29) kattu (to build)

Pronoun	Past	Translation	Present Continuous	Translation
nenu (I)	kattaanu	I built	kaduthunnaanu	I am building
nuvvu (You) (imp)	kattaavu	You built	kaduthunnaavu	You are building
miiru (You) (polite)	kattaaru	You built	kaduthunnaaru	You are building
aayana (He) (polite)		He built		He is building
aavida (She) (polite)		She built		She is building
vaaLLu (They)		They built		They are building
athanu (He) (impolite)	kattaadu	He built	kaduthunnaadu	He is building
meemu (We) (inclusive)	kattaamu	We built	kaduthunnaamu	We are building
manamu (We) (exclusive)	kattaamu	We built	kaduthunnaamu	We are building
aame/adhi/idhi	kattindhi	She, that, this built	kaduthundhi	She/that/this is building
avi/ivi (Those/These)	kattaayi	These, those built	kaduthunnaayi	Those/These are building

30) thittu (to scold)

Pronoun	Past	Translation	Present Continuous	Translation
nenu (I)	thittaanu	I scolded	thiduthunnaanu	I am scolding
nuvvu (You) (imp)	thittaavu	You scolded	thiduthunnaavu	You are scolding
miiru (You) (polite)	thittaaru	You scolded	thiduthunnaaru	You are scolding
aayana (He) (polite)		He scolded		He is scolding
aavida (She) (polite)		She scolded		She is scolding
vaaLLu (They)		They scolded		They are scolding
athanu (He) (impolite)	thittaadu	He scolded	thiduthunnaadu	He is scolding
meemu (We) (incl)	thittaamu	We scolded	thiduthunnaamu	We are scolding
manamu (We) (excl)	thittaamu	We scolded	thiduthunnaamu	We are scolding
aame/adhi/idhi	thittindhi	She, that, this scolded	thiduthundhi	She/that/this is scolding
avi/ivi (Those/These)	thittaayi	These, those scolded	thiduthunnaayi	Those/These are scolding

Pronoun	Future	Translation
nenu (I)	thidathaanu	I will scold
nuvvu (You) (impolite)	thidathaavu	You will scold
miiru (You) (polite)	thidathaadu	You will scold
aayana (He) (polite)		He will scold
aavida (She) (polite)		She will scold
vaaLLu (They)		They will scold
athanu (He) (impolite)	thidathaadu	He will scold
meemu (We) (inclusive)	thidathaamu	We will scold
manamu (We) (exclusive)	thidathaamu	We will scold
aame/adhi/idhi	thidathundhi	She/that/this will scold
avi/ivi (Those/These)	thidathaayi	Those/These will scold

31) pettu (to keep / put)

Pronoun	Past	Translation	Present Continuous	Translation
nenu (I)	pettaanu	I kept	peduthunnaanu	I am keeping
nuvvu (You) (imp)	pettaavu	You kept	peduthunnaavu	You are keeping
miiru (You) (polite)	pettaaru	You kept	peduthunnaaru	You are keeping
aayana (He) (polite)		He kept		He is keeping
aavida (She) (polite)		She kept		She is keeping
vaaLLu (They)		They kept		They are keeping
athanu (He) (impolite)	pettaadu	He kept	peduthunnaadu	He is keeping
meemu (We) (incl)	pettaamu	We kept	peduthunnaamu	We are keeping
manamu (We) (excl)	pettaamu	We kept	peduthunnaamu	We are keeping
aame/adhi/idhi	pettindhi	She, that, this kept	peduthundhi	She/that/this is keeping
avi/ivi (Those/These)	pettaayi	These, those kept	peduthunnaayi	Those/These are keeping

Pronoun	Future	Translation
nenu (I)	pedathaanu	I will keep
nuvvu (You) (impolite)	pedathaavu	You will keep
miiru (You) (polite)	pedathaadu	You will keep
aayana (He) (polite)		He will keep
aavida (She) (polite)		She will keep
vaaLLu (They)		They will keep
athanu (He) (impolite)	pedathaadu	He will keep
meemu (We) (inclusive)	pedathaamu	We will keep
manamu (We) (exclusive)	pedathaamu	We will keep
aame/adhi/idhi	peduthundhi	She/that/this will keep
avi/ivi (Those/These)	pedathaayi	Those/These will keep

32) kottu (to hit)

Pronoun	Past	Translation	Present Continuous	Translation
nenu (I)	kottaanu	I hit	koduthunnaanu	I am hitting
nuvvu (You) (imp)	kottaavu	You hit	koduthunnaavu	You are hitting
miiru (You) (polite)	kottaaru	You hit	koduthunnaaru	You are hitting
aayana (He) (polite)		He hit		He is hitting
aavida (She) (polite)		She hit		She is hitting
vaaLLu (They)		They hit		They are hitting
athanu (He) (impolite)	kottaadu	He hit	koduthunnaadu	He is hitting
meemu (We) (incl)	kottaamu	We hit	koduthunnaamu	We are hitting
manamu (We) (excl)	kottaamu	We hit	koduthunnaamu	We are hitting
aame/adhi/idhi	kottindhi	She, that, this hit	koduthundhi	She/that/this is hitting
avi/ivi (Those/These)	kottaayi	These, those hit	koduthunnaayi	Those/These are hitting

Pronoun	Future	Translation
nenu (I)	kodathaanu	I will hit
nuvvu (You) (impolite)	kodathaavu	You will hit
miiru (You) (polite)	kodathaadu	You will hit
aayana (He) (polite)		He will hit
aavida (She) (polite)		She will hit
vaaLLu (They)		They will hit
athanu (He) (impolite)	kodathaadu	He will hit
meemu (We) (inclusive)	kodathaamu	We will hit
manamu (We) (exclusive)	kodathaamu	We will hit
aame/adhi/idhi	koduthundhi	She/that/this will hit
avi/ivi (Those/These)	kodathaayi	Those/These will hit

Class 8 verbs

In class 8 verbs, you will replace the ending of the root verb 'ko' with 'kunn' while conjugating the verb in all the past tense and with 'kun' while conjugating the verb in present continuous and future tense.

Example: Class 8 root verb "aaduko" (to play)

nenu (aaduko + -aa + -nu) = nenu aadukunnaanu (I played) (Past)

nenu (aaduko + -tunnaa + -nu) = nenu aadukuntunnaanu (I am playing) (continuous)

nenu (aaduko + -taa + -nu) = nenu aadukuntaanu (I will play) (Future)

33) aaduko (to play)

Pronoun	Past	Translation	Present Continuous	Translation
nenu (I)	aadukunnaanu	I played	aadukuntunaanu	I am playing
nuvvu (You)	aadukunnaavu	You played	aadukuntunnaavu	You are playing
miiru (You) (polite)	aadukunnaru	You played	aadukuntunaaru	You are playing
aayana (He) (polite)		He played		He is playing
aavida (She) (polite)		She played		She is playing
vaaLLu (They)		They played		They are playing
athanu (He) (impolite)	aadukunnaadu	He played	aadukuntunnaadu	He is playing
meemu (We) (inclusive)	aadukunnaamu	We played	aadukuntunnaamu	We are playing
manamu (We) (exclusive)	aadukunnaamu	We played	aadukuntunnaamu	We are playing
aame/adhi/idhi	aadukundhi	She, that, this played	aadukuntundhi	She/that/this is playing
avi/ivi (Those/These)	aadukunnaayi	These, those played	aadukuntunnaayi	Those/These are playing

34) paduko (to lie down)

Pronoun	Past	Translation
nenu (I)	padukunnaanu	I lay down
nuvvu (You) (impolite)	padukunnaavu	You lay down
miiru (You) (polite)	padukunnaru	You lay down
aayana (He) (polite)		He lay down
aavida (She) (polite)		She lay down
vaaLLu (They)		They lay down
athanu (He)	padukunnaadu	He lay down
meemu (We) (inclusive)	padukunnaamu	We lay down
manamu (We) (exclusive)	padukunnaamu	We lay down
aame/adhi/idhi	padukundhi	She, that, this lay down
avi/ivi (Those/These)	padukunnaayi	These, those lay down

Pronoun	Present Continuous	Translation
nenu (I)	padukuntunaanu	I am lying down
nuvvu (You) (impolite)	padukuntunnaavu	You are lying down
miiru (You) (polite)	padukuntunaaru	You are lying down
aayana (He) (polite)		He is lying down
aavida (She) (polite)		She is lying down
vaaLLu (They)		They are lying down
athanu (He)	padukuntunnaadu	He is lying down
meemu (We) (inclusive)	padukuntunnaamu	We are lying down
manamu (We) (exclusive)	padukuntunnaamu	We are lying down
aame/adhi/idhi	padukuntundhi	She/that/this is lying down
avi/ivi (Those/These)	padukuntunnaayi	Those/These are lying down

Pronoun	Future	Translation
nenu (I)	padukuntaanu	I will lie down
nuvvu (You) (impolite)	padukuntaavu	You will lie down
miiru (You) (polite)	padukuntaaru	You will lie down
aayana (He) (polite)		He will lie down
aavida (She) (polite)		She will lie down
vaaLLu (They)		They will lie down
athanu (He) (impolite)	padukuntaadu	He will lie down
meemu (We) (inclusive)	padukuntaamu	We will lie down
manamu (We) (exclusive)	padukuntaamu	We will lie down
aame/adhi/idhi	padukuntundhi	She/that/this will lie down
avi/ivi (Those/These)	padukuntaayi	Those/These will lie down

35) nerchuko (to learn)

Pronoun	Past	Translation
nenu (I)	nerchukunnaanu	I learnt
nuvvu (You) (impolite)	nerchukunnaavu	You learnt
miiru (You) (polite)	nerchukunnaru	You learnt
aayana (He) (polite)		He learnt
aavida (She) (polite)		She learnt
vaaLLu (They)		They learnt
athanu (He) (impolite)	nerchukunnaadu	He learnt
meemu (We) (inclusive)	nerchukunnaamu	We learnt
manamu (We) (exclusive)	nerchukunnaamu	We learnt
aame/adhi/idhi	nerchukundhi	She, that, this learnt
avi/ivi (Those/These)	nerchukunnaayi	These, those learnt

Pronoun	Present Continuous	Translation
nenu (I)	nerchukuntunaanu	I am learning
nuvvu (You) (impolite)	nerchukuntunnaavu	You are learning
miiru (You) (polite)	nerchukuntunaaru	You are learning
aayana (He) (polite)		He is learning
aavida (She) (polite)		She is learning
vaaLLu (They)		They are learning
athanu (He) (impolite)	nerchukuntunnaadu	He is learning
meemu (We) (inclusive)	nerchukuntunnaamu	We are learning
manamu (We) (exclusive)	nerchukuntunnaamu	We are learning
aame/adhi/idhi	nerchukuntundhi	She/that/this is learning
avi/ivi (Those/These)	nerchukuntunnaayi	Those/These are learning

Pronoun	Future	Translation
nenu (I)	nerchukuntaanu	I will learn
nuvvu (You) (impolite)	nerchukuntaavu	You will learn
miiru (You) (polite)	nerchukuntaaru	You will learn
aayana (He) (polite)		He will learn
aavida (She) (polite)		She will learn
vaaLLu (They)		They will learn
athanu (He) (impolite)	nerchukuntaadu	He will learn
meemu (We) (inclusive)	nerchukuntaamu	We will learn
manamu (We) (exclusive)	nerchukuntaamu	We will learn
aame/adhi/idhi	nerchukuntundhi	She/that/this will learn
avi/ivi (Those/These)	nerchukuntaayi	Those/These will call

Word Order in Telugu:

The standard word order in a sentence in Telugu is "Subject Object Verb" (SOV); it is completely opposite to the word order in English (SVO). There may be some sentences in Telugu where the word order is different, but it doesn't matter, because in Telugu you have greater flexibility towards word order. You have all the freedom to change the word order to some extent.

In English, you don't have such freedom; you have to always follow the rule "Subject Verb Object" otherwise the entire sentence will be meaningless. But in Telugu, you can move them around; most of the time it will give you the same meaning but sometimes it may change the meaning of the sentence. Reason being that while you reorder the sentences, you may end up giving more importance to another word instead of the one you intend to.

Note: Not all Telugu sentences have subjects, verbs, and objects.

Word order in Telugu also comes with small rules like; modifying words such as adjectives and adverbs always precede the word that they modify, but an adverb which is not a modifier of an adjective or adverb can be reordered.

Note: In most of the sentences in Telugu, the verb usually comes at the end.

Example:

a) I am in the shop. (The below two sentences means the same in Telugu)

nenu shoplo untunnaanu (lt: I am in the shop)

shoplo nenu untunnaanu (lt: in the shop I am)

b) Shall we go to the shop? (The below two sentences means the same in Telugu)

shopki meemu veLthaamaa? (lt: to the shop shall we go?)

meemu veLthaamaa shopki? (lt: shall we go to the shop)

c) When shall we go to the shop? (The below three sentences means the same in Telugu).

shopki eppudu meemu veLthaamu? (lt: to the shop when shall we go?).

eppudu meemu veLthaamu shopki (lt: when shall we go to the shop?).

eppudu shopki meemu veLthaamu (lit: when to the shop shall we go?).

As you saw in the above example, all of them are correct irrespective of their word order. But like I mentioned earlier, modifying words like adjective and adverb will always precede the word that they modify, but an adverb which is not a modifier of an adjective or adverb can be reordered.

Example:

aayana ki okka eruppu car undhi (he has a red car) - Correct

Here eruppu (red) is an Adjective of the noun 'car', so one should always use "eruppu car" while forming a sentence; it should never change position.

aayana ki eruppu okka car undhi - This sentence is wrong because you cannot split the adjective from the noun, hence it is wrong.

Important Note:

Verb Classes in this chapter is simply a workaround for the indescribable changes in the verb root while conjugating the verb root, because basically in Telugu, a verb belongs to a particular class because they are and there is no other explanation for it.

Hence, we tried to find a pattern (like a pattern due to coincidence), and we were able to find a pattern for most of the classes. Using these verb class examples given in this chapter, you can figure out the Present tense, Past tense, and Future tense of a verb. The chances of figuring it out right is approximately 60-70%, because we still have some exceptions.

It is little difficult, but Present tense, Present Continuous tense and Future tense of a verb is very important as we use them while creating almost every sentence in Telugu. So, you have to understand them and form them, there is no other choice.But you can follow one of the following methods that I have given below to form the perfect verb conjugation.

Method 1: You can use the Verb class examples that I have provided in this chapter.

Advantages: This method is easier and less time consuming, as all you have to do is just memorize the pattern and remember it whenever you need to form a sentence using tenses; then you are good.

Drawbacks:

a. since they work only on approx. 60-70% of verbs, there will be some verbs where you will have to memorize them as it is.

b. As you are memorizing the verb class table, every time when you want to form a sentence in Telugu and you come across a tense in that sentence, then you will have to look into these examples to find them. This will cause dependency on them and you will also stammer while talking in Telugu as you have to do a lot of thinking while putting together a sentence.

Method 2: In the next chapter, I will be providing top commonly used verbs in Telugu, also their verb conjugation with all three tenses. You have to memorize all of them, practice using them in small sentences and know them by heart.

Advantages:

a. this method is very traditional and effective; you will be able to form sentences using these verbs almost instantly, as you will know them by heart.

b. Similar to the Verb class given in this chapter, all verbs have a pattern and that's how Telugu native speakers remember the Tense stem. So, once you memorize these common Verbs and use them in sentences, you will be able to predict even verbs which are not available in these common verbs list you memorized.

Drawbacks: Time consuming.

Note: I would personally recommend you go for method two. I know it's time consuming, but it is the best way and will help you a lot to speak Telugu in the long run; but it's up to you, you can choose which ever method you feel comfortable with.

Exercises:

C) Translate the following from English to Telugu.

Words to help you in these exercise: rat = yeluka, in = lo, this side = i vaipu, that side = a vaipu, left side = yedama vaipu , right side = kudi vaipu , kill = champu, cry = yeduvu, laugh or smile = navvu, turn or wander = thirugu, sit = kuurcho, okka = a, one.

1. I killed a rat

2. I am smiling

3. I wandered in the mall

4. I sat in the train

5. Please turn to this side

6. Please smile

7. She is crying (Polite and impolite)

8. Are you crying? (Polite and impolite)

9. Did you cry? (Polite and impolite)

10. Turn to the left side

11. Please turn to the right side

12. Did you sit in the park?

D) Match the following.

Telugu	English
1. yeluka	a. Smile
2. navvu	b. Rat
3. yedupu	c. Turn
4. thirugu	d. Right side
5. i vaipu	e. Left side
6. a vaipu	f. This side
7. kudi vaipu	g. That side
8. yedama vaipu	h. Cry

E) Translate the following from English to Telugu.

Words to help you in these exercises: to do = cheyyi, to wake up or to rise up = le, to come = vochcha, to go = veLLu, to drive = nadupu, to walk = naduvu, to = ki, cat = pilli, cats = pillulu, podhdhuna = morning, now = ippudu, yesterday = ninna, today = i roju.

1. Did you do the homework? (Casual)

2. Did she drive the car?

3. I am driving the car

4. They are walking

5. Those cats are walking

6. Are these cats walking?

7. Will you come to Chennai?

8. They are going to the park

9. I woke up now

10. Please get up

11. They went today

12. She is going now

13. She went yesterday

14. I am going today afternoon

F) Match the following.

English	Telugu
1. to	a. madhyanam
2. cat	b. ninna
3. morning	c. ippudu
4. now	d. raathri
5. afternoon	e. i roju
6. night	f. podhdhuna
7. today	g. pilli
8. yesterday	h. ki

G) Translate the following from English to Telugu.

Words to help you in these exercises: in = lo, umbrella = godugu, milk = paalu, book = pusthakam, salt = uppu, vegetables = kuuragaayalu, to take = thiisko, to give = ivvu, niillu = water, manchi = good.

1. I slept.

2. Did you take the vegetables?

3. Please drink coffee

4. Please take umbrella

5. Did you drink coffee?

6. Did they gave chocolates?

7. Please take the note book

8. Will he cut the vegetables?

9. Did you put salt in the salad?

10. Will they read the books?

11. Did it drank milk?

12. I am writing home work

13. Please give drinking/good water

14. They will read the book

15. I gave the umbrella

H) Match the following.

English	Telugu
1. in	a. kuuragayalu
2. umbrella	b. paalu
3. milk	c. uppu
4. notebook	d. lo
5. salt	e. godugu
6. vegetables	f. pusthakam

Solutions

Exercise A

1) vaallu ippudu bhojanam thintunnaaru 2) aavida ice cream thinnaaru 3) meemu / manamu ninna ice cream thinnaamu 4) miiru Ice cream thintaaru 5) athanu Ice cream thintunnaadu 6) aame ice cream thintundhi 7) vaallu ice cream thintunnaaru

Exercise B

1a & b) muyyi (to close)

Pronoun	Present Continuous	Translation	Future	Translation
nenu (I)	musthunnaanu	I am closing	musthaanu	I will close
nuvvu (You) (imp)	musthunnaavu	You are closing	musthaavu	You will close
miiru (You) (polite)	musthunnaaru	You are closing	musthaaru	You will close
aayana (He) (polite)		He is closing		He will close
aavida (She) (polite)		She is closing		She will close
vaaLLu (They)		They are closing		They will close
athanu (He) (impolite)	musthunaadu	He is closing	musthaadu	He will close
meemu (We) (incl)	musthunaamu	We are closing	musthaamu	We will close
manamu (We) (excl)	musthunaamu	We are closing	musthaamu	We will close
aame/adhi/idhi	musthundhi	She/that/this is closing	musthundhi	She/that/this will close
avi/ivi (Those/These)	musthunnaayi	Those/These are closing	musthaayi	Those/These will close

2a, b & c) kanapadu (to be able to see)

Pronoun	Present Continuous	Translation	Future
nenu (I)	kanapaduthunnaanu	I am able to see	kanapaduthaanu
nuvvu (You) (imp)	kanapaduthunnavu	You are able to see	kanapaduthaavu
miiru (You) (polite)	kanapaduthunnaru	You are able to see	kanapaduthaaru
aayana (He) (polite)		He is able to see	
aavida (She) (polite)		She is able to see	
vaaLLu (They)		They are able to see	
athanu (He)	kanapaduthunnadu	He is able to see	kanapaduthaadu
meemu (We) (incl)	kanapaduthunnaamu	We are able to see	kanapaduthaamu
manamu (We) (excl)	kanapaduthunnaamu	We are able to see	kanapaduthaamu
aame/adhi/idhi	kanapaduthundhi	She/that/this is able to see	kanapaduthundhi
avi/ivi (Those/These)	kanapaduthunnaayi	Those/These are able to see	kanapaduthaayi

3a, b & c) nimpu (to fill)

Pronoun	Past	Translation	Present Continuous	Translation
nenu (I)	nimpaanu	I filled	nimputhunaanu	I am filling
nuvvu (You) (imp)	nimpaavu	You filled	nimputhunaavu	You are filling
miiru (You) (polite)	nimpaaru	You filled	nimputhunaaru	You are filling
aayana (He) (polite)		He filled		He is filling
aavida (She) (polite)		She filled		She is filling
vaaLLu (They)		They filled		They are filling
athanu (He) (impolite)	nimpaadu	He filled	nimputhunnaadu	He is filling
meemu (We) (incl)	nimpaamu	We filled	nimputhunaamu	We are filling
manamu (We) (excl)	nimpaamu	We filled	nimputhunaamu	We are filling
aame/adhi/idhi	nimpindhi	She, that, this filled	nimputhundhi	She/that/this is filling
avi/ivi (Those/These)	nimpaayi	These, those filled	nimputhunnaayi	Those/These are filling

Pronoun	Future	Translation
nenu (I)	nimputhaanu	I will fill
nuvvu (You) (impolite)	nimputhaavu	You will fill
miiru (You) (polite)	nimputhaaru	You will fill
aayana (He) (polite)		He will fill
aavida (She) (polite)		She will fill
vaaLLu (They)		They will fill
athanu (He) (impolite)	nimputhaadu	He will fill
meemu (We) (inclusive)	nimputhaamu	We will fill
manamu (We) (exclusive)	nimputhaamu	We will fill
aame/adhi/idhi	nimputhundhi	She/that/this will fill
avi/ivi (Those/These)	nimputhaayi	Those/These will fill

4a, b & c) pampu (to send)

Pronoun	Past	Translation	Present Continuous	Translation
nenu (I)	pampaanu	I sent	pamputhunaanu	I am sending
nuvvu (You) (imp)	pampaavu	You sent	pamputhunaavu	You are sending
miiru (You) (polite)	pampaaru	You sent	pamputhunaaru	You are sending
aayana (He) (polite)		He sent		He is sending
aavida (She) (polite)		She sent		She is sending
vaaLLu (They)		They sent		They are sending
athanu (He) (impolite)	pampaadu	He sent	pamputhunnaadu	He is sending
meemu (We) (incl)	pampaamu	We sent	pamputhunaamu	We are sending
manamu (We) (excl)	pampaamu	We sent	pamputhunaamu	We are sending
aame/adhi/idhi	pampindhi	She, that, this sent	pamputhundhi	She/that/this is sending
avi/ivi (Those/These)	pampaayi	These, those sent	pamputhunnaayi	Those/These are sending

Pronoun	Future	Translation
nenu (I)	pamputhaanu	I will send
nuvvu (You) (impolite)	pamputhaavu	You will send
miiru (You) (polite)	pamputhaaru	You will send
aayana (He) (polite)		He will send
aavida (She) (polite)		She will send
vaaLLu (They)		They will send
athanu (He) (impolite)	pamputhaadu	He will send
meemu (We) (inclusive)	pamputhaamu	We will send
manamu (We) (exclusive)	pamputhaamu	We will send
aame/adhi/idhi	pamputhundhi	She/that/this will send
avi/ivi (Those/These)	pamputhaayi	Those/These will send

5a, b & c) chupinchu (to show)

Pronoun	Past	Translation	Present Continuous	Translation
nenu (I)	chupinchaanu	I showed	chupisthunnaanu	I am showing
nuvvu (You) (imp)	chupinchaavu	You showed	chupisthunnaavu	You are showing
miiru (You) (polite)	chupinchaaru	You showed	chupisthunnaaru	You are showing
aayana (He) (polite)		He showed		He is showing
aavida (She) (polite)		She showed		She is showing
vaaLLu (They)		They showed		They are showing
athanu (He)	chupinchaadu	He showed	chupisthunnaadu	He is showing
meemu (We) (incl)	chupinchaamu	We showed	chupisthunnaamu	We are showing
manamu (We) (excl)	chupinchaamu	We showed	chupisthunnaamu	We are showing
aame/adhi/idhi	chupinchindhi	She, that, this showed	chupisthundhi	She/that/this is showing
avi/ivi (Those/These)	chupinchaayi	These, those showed	chupisthunnaayi	Those/These are showing

Pronoun	Future	Translation
nenu (I)	chupisthaanu	I will show
nuvvu (You) (impolite)	chupisthaavu	You will show
miiru (You) (polite)	chupisthaaru	You will show
aayana (He) (polite)		He will show
aavida (She) (polite)		She will show
vaaLLu (They)		They will show
athanu (He) (impolite)	chupisthaadu	He will show
meemu (We) (inclusive)	chupisthaamu	We will show
manamu (We) (exclusive)	chupisthaamu	We will show
aame/adhi/idhi	chupisthundhi	She/that/this will show
avi/ivi (Those/These)	chupisthaayi	Those/These will show

6a, b & c) vochcha (to come)

Pronoun	Past	Translation	Present Continuous	Translation
nenu (I)	vochchaanu	I came	vochchesthunnaanu	I am coming
nuvvu (You) (imp)	vochchaavu	You came	vochchesthunnaavu	You are coming
miiru (You) (polite)	vochchaaru	You came	vochchesthunnaaru	You are coming
aayana (He) (polite)		He came		He is coming
aavida (She) (polite)		She came		She is coming
vaaLLu (They)		They came		They are coming
athanu (He)	vochchaadu	He came	vochchesthunnaadu	He is coming
meemu (We) (incl)	vochchaamu	We came	vochchesthunnaamu	We are coming
manamu (We) (excl)	vochchaamu	We came	vochchesthunnaamu	We are coming
aame/adhi/idhi	vochchindhi	She, that, this came	vochchesthundhi	She/that/this is coming
avi/ivi (Those/These)	vochchaayi	These, those came	vochchesthunnaayi	Those/These are coming

Pronoun	Future	Translation
nenu (I)	vochchesthaanu	I will come
nuvvu (You) (impolite)	vochchesthaavu	You will come
miiru (You) (polite)	vochchesthaaru	You will come
aayana (He) (polite)		He will come
aavida (She) (polite)		She will come
vaaLLu (They)		They will come
athanu (He) (impolite)	vochchesthaadu	He will come
meemu (We) (inclusive)	vochchesthaamu	We will come
manamu (We) (exclusive)	vochchesthaamu	We will come
aame/adhi/idhi	vochchesthundhi	She/that/this will come
avi/ivi (Those/These)	vochchesthaayi	Those/These will come

Exercise C

1) nenu okka yelukanu champaanu. 2) nenu navvuthunaanu. 3) nenu mall lo thirigaanu. 4) nenu train lo kuurchunnaanu. 5) i vaipu thiragandi. 6) navvandi 7) aame yeedusthundhi or aavida yedusthunaaru. 8) miiru yedusthunnaaraa? or nuvvu yedusthunnaavaa? 9) nuvvu yedichaavaa? or miiru yedichaaraa? 10) yedama vaipu thirugu. 11) kudi vaipu thiragandi. 12) park lo kuuchunnaavaa?

Exercise D

1) b, 2) a, 3) h, 4) c, 5) f, 6) g, 7) d, 8) e.

Exercise E

1) nuvvu homework chesaavaa? 2) aame car nadipindhaa? 3) nenu car naduputhunnaanu 4) vaaLLu nadusthunnaaru 5) avi pillili nadusthunnaayi 6) avi pillili nadusthunnaayaa? 7) nuvvu Chennai ki vochchesthaavaa? 8) vaaLLu park ki veLthunnaaru 9) nenu ippudu lesaanu/lechaanu 10) miiru dhayacheesi leyyandi (super polite), miiru leyyandi (polite) 11) vaaLLu I roju veLLaaru 12) aame ippudu veLthundhi 13) aame ninna veLLindhi 14) nenu I roju madhyanam veLthunnaanu.

Exercise F

1) h, 2) g, 3) f, 4) c, 5) a, 6) d, 7) e, 8) b.

Exercise G

1) nenu padukunnaanu 2) nuvvu salad thiiskunnavaa? 3) coffee thaagandi 4) godugu thiiskoandi 5) miiru coffee thaagaara? 6) vaaLLu chocolates ichaaraa? 7) pusthakam thiisuku andi 8) athanu vegetables kosthaadaa? 9) salad lo uppu vesaaraa? 10) vaaLLu pusthakaalu chadhuvuthaaraa? 11) adhi paalu thaagindhaa? 12) nenu homework raasthunnaanu 13) manchi niillu ivvandi 14) vaaLLu pusthakam chadhuvuthaaru 15) nenu godugu ichaanu.

Exercise H

1) d, 2) e, 3) b, 4) f, 5) c, 6) a.

LESSON 6: COMMONLY USED TELUGU VERBS

In the table below, you will find 75 commonly used verbs in Telugu with their conjugation form for 'nenu' (I) in past, present continuous and future tense. The reason why I gave the conjugation form only for 'nenu' (I) is that the rest of the verb conjugation for other pronouns would be the same but with a different ending based on their pronouns, that's it. So, simply learn the verb conjugation for one pronoun and you will be able to make the verb conjugation for other pronouns all by yourself.

Example: Verb root: veLLu (to go)

	Verb	English	Past tense	Continuous tense	Future tense
8	veLLu	To go	veLLaanu	veLthunnaanu	veLthaanu
			I went	I am going	I will go

nenu veLLaanu - I went (past)

nenu veLthunnaanu - I am going (Present continuous)

nenu veLthaanu - I will go (Future)

Since you have already learned the above form, you will be able to use this conjugation for other pronouns as well.

For example: Let's say you want to conjugate the verb root 'veLLu' (to go), to make the sentence "we will go" in Telugu. You just have to use the above as a reference and change the pronoun and the conjugated verb ending. Look below for more clarity.

manamu veLthaamu - we will go (Future)

In the above sentence structure, all I did was "I changed the pronoun 'nenu' (I) to 'manamu' (we) and changed the conjugated verb ending from '-nu' to '-mu'.

That's it; you will be able to do the same for almost every pronoun except 'aame/adhi/idhi (she/that/this)'. For this, it's much simpler, you just have to add the suffix '-indhi' for past tense and '-thundhi' for present continuous and future tense.

With this concept you will be able to learn common verbs and their conjugations with pronouns in Telugu, which will help you to make sentences easily in Telugu.

As mentioned above, kindly find the below tables with 75 verbs in Telugu in the Past, Present continuous and Future tense form for the pronoun 'nenu'.

	Verb	English	Past tense	Continuous tense	Future tense
1	undhu	To be / have	unnaanu	untunnaanu	untaanu
			I was	I am	I will be
2	cheyyi	To do	chesaanu	chesthunaanu	chesthaanu
			I did	I am doing	I will do
3	saadhinchu	To achive	saadhinchaanu	saadhisthunaanu	saadhisthaanu
			I achieved	I am achieving	I will achieve
4	thirugu	To wander	thirigaanu	thiruguthunnaanu	thiruguthaanu
			I wandered	I am wandering	I will wander
5	kuurcho	To sit	kuurchunnaanu	kuurchuntunnaanu	kuurchuntaanu
			I sat	I am sitting	I will sit
6	le	To raise / get up	lechaanu	lesthunnaanu	lesthaanu
			I got up	I am getting up	I will get up
7	vochcha	To come	vochchaanu	vosthunaannu	vosthaanu
			I came	I am coming	I will come
8	veLLlu	To go	veLLaanu	veLthunnaanu	veLthaanu
			I went	I am going	I will go
9	bratuku	To survive	bratikaanu	bratukuthunnaanu	bratukuthaanu
			I survived	I am surviving	I will survive
10	padu	To fall	paddaanu	paduthunnaanu	padathaanu
			I fell	I am falling	I will fall

	Verb	English	Past tense	Continuous tense	Future tense
11	avvu	To become	ayyanu	avuthunnaanu	avuthaanu
			I became	I am becoming	I will become
12	aaduko	To play	aadukunnaanu	aadukuntunnaanu	aadukuntaanu
			I played	I am playing	I will play
13	poyyi	To pour	posaanu	posthunnaanu	posthaanu
			I poured	I am pouring	I will pour
14	raayi	To write	raasaanu	raasthunnaanu	raasthaanu
			I wrote	I am writing	I will write
15	parigeththu	To run	parigettaanu	parigeduthunnaanu	parigeduthaanu
			I ran	I am running	I will run
16	nadupu	To drive	nadipaanu	naduputhunnaanu	naduputhaanu
			I drove	I am driving	I will drive
17	vesko	To wear	veskunnaanu	veskuntunaanu	veskuntaanu
			I wore	I am wearing	I will wear
18	kattu	To build, to tie	kattanu	kaduthunnaanu	kadathaanu
			I built	I am building	I will build, tie
19	aruvu	To scream	arichaanu	arusthunnaanu	arusthaanu
			I screamed	I am screaming	I will scream
20	kadugu	To wash	kadigaanu	kaduguthunnanu	kaduguthaanu
			I washed	I am washing	I will wash
21	thuduvu	To wipe	thudichchaanu	thudusthunnaanu	thudusthaanu
			I wiped	I am wiping	I will wipe

	Verb	English	Past tense	Continuous tense	Future tense
22	uthuku	To wash clothes	uthikaanu	uthukuthunnaanu	uthukuthaanu
			I washed clothes	I am washing clothes	I will wash clothes
23	thiisei	To remove	thiisesaanu	thiisesthunnaanu	thiisesthaanu
			I removed	I am removing	I will remove
24	dhuvvu	To comb	dhuvvaanu	dhuvvuthunnaanu	dhuvvuthaanu
			I combed	I am combing	I will comb
25	nettu	To push	nettaanu	neduthunnaanu	nedathaanu
			I pushed	I am pushing	I will push
26	kottu	To hit	kottaanu	koduthunnaanu	kodathaanu
			I hit	I am hitting	I will hit
27	vethuku	To search	vethikaanu	vethukuthunnaanu	vethukuthaanu
			I searched	I am searching	I will search
28	nammu	To believe	nammanu	nammuthunnaanu	nammuthaanu
			I believed	I am believing	I will believe
29	doraku	To get	dorikaanu	dorukuthunnaanu	dorukuthaanu
			I got	I am getting	I will get
30	vaadu	To use	vaadaanu	vaaduthunnaanu	vaaduthaanu
			I used	I am using	I will use
31	paadu	To sing	paadaanu	paaduthunnaanu	paaduthaanu
			I sang	I am singing	I will sing
32	matlaadu	To speak	matlaadaanu	matlaaduthunnaanu	matlaaduthaanu
			I spoke	I am speaking	I will speak

	Verb	English	Past tense	Continuous tense	Future tense
33	matlaadu	To speak	matlaadaanu	matlaaduthunnaanu	matlaaduthaanu
			I spoke	I am speaking	I will speak
34	muyyi	To close	musaanu	musthunnaanu	musthaanu
			I closed	I am closing	I will close
35	konu	To buy	konnaanu	kontunnaanu	kontaanu
			I bought	I am buying	I will buy
36	ammu	To sell	ammaanu	ammuthunnaanu	ammuthaanu
			I sold	I am selling	I will sell
37	ventapadu	To chase	ventapaddanu	ventapaduthunnaanu	ventapduthaanu
			I chased	I am chasing	I will chase
38	piluvu	To call	pilichaanu	pilusthunnaanu	pilusthaanu
			I called	I am calling	I will call
39	thinu	To eat	thinnaanu	thintunnaaanu	thintaanu
			I ate	I am eating	I will eat
40	kaalchu	To shoot	kaalchaanu	kaalusthunnaanu	kaalusthaanu
			I shot	I am shooting	I will shoot
41	cheppu	To tell	cheppaanu	chepthunnaanu	chepthaanu
			I told	I am telling	I will tell
42	thadumu	To touch	thadimaanu	thadumuthunnaanu	thadumthaanu
			I touched	I am touching	I will touch
43	vodhilai	To leave	vodhilesaanu	vodhilesthunnaanu	vodhilesthaanu
			I left	I am leaving	I will leave

	Verb	English	Past tense	Continuous tense	Future tense
44	nilabadu	To stand	nilabaddaanu	nilabaduthunnaanu	nilabaduthaanu
			I stood	I am standing	I will stand
45	chuudu	To see	chusaanu	chusthunnanu	chusthaanu
			I saw	I am seeing	I will see
46	chupinchu	To show	chupinchaanu	chupisthunnaanu	chupisthaanu
			I showed	I am showing	I will show
47	pettu	To keep	pettaanu	peduthunnaanu	pedthaanu
			I kept	I am keeping	I will keep
48	chadhuvu	To read	chadhivaanu	chadhuvuthunnaanu	chadhuvuthaanu
			I read	I am reading	I will read
49	nerchuko	To learn	nerchukunnaanu	nerchukuntunaanu	nerchukuntaanu
			I learnt	I am learning	I will learn
50	nerpinchu	To teach	nerpinchaanu	nerpisthunnaanu	nerpisthaanu
			I taught	I am teaching	I will teach
51	natinchu	To act	natinchaanu	natisthunnaanu	natisthaanu
			I acted	I am acting	I will act
52	thiisko	To take	thiiskunnaanu	thiiskunthunnaanu	thiiskunthaanu
			I took	I am taking	I will take
53	thiiskura	To bring along	thiiskochaanu	thiikosthunnaanu	thiiskosthaanu
			I brought along	I am bringing along	I will bring along

	Verb	English	Past tense	Continuous tense	Future tense
54	thiiskuvellu	To take away	thiiskuvellanu	thiiskuvelthunnaanu	thiiskuvelthaanu
			I took away	I am taking away	I will take away
55	pattuko	To hold	pattukunnaanu	pattukunthunnaanu	pattukunthaanu
			I holded	I am holding	I will hold
56	maduvu	To fold	madichaanu	madusthunnaanu	madusthaanu
			I folded	I am folding	I will fold
57	thaagu	To drink	thaagaanu	thaaguthunnaanu	thaaguthaanu
			I drank	I am drinking	I will drink
58	vondu	To cook	vondaanu	vonduthunnaanu	vonduthaanu
			I cooked	I am cooking	I will cook
59	laagu	To pull	laagaanu	laaguthunnaanu	laaguthaanu
			I pulled	I am pulling	I will pull
60	gamaninchu	To observe	gamaninchaanu	gamanisthunnaanu	gamanisthaanu
			I observed	I am observing	I will observe
61	navvu	To laugh	navvaanu	navvuthunnaanu	navvuthaanu
			I laughed	I am laughing	I will laugh
62	naduvu	To walk	nadichaanu	nadustunnanau	nadusthaanu
			I walked	I am walking	I will walk
63	marchipo	To forget	machipoyaanu	marchipothunnaanu	marchipothaanu
			I forgot	I am forgeting	I will forget
64	theruvu	To open	therichaanu	therusthunaanu	therusthaanu
			I opened	I am opening	I will open

	Verb	English	Past tense	Continuous tense	Future tense
65	yeghuru	To fly	yeghiraanu	yeghuruthunnaanu	yeghuruthaanu
			I flew	I am flying	I will fly
66	chachipo	To die	chachipoyaanu	chachipothunnaanu	chachipothaanu
			I died	I am dying	I will die
67	kalupu	To mix	kalipaanu	kaluputhunnaanu	kaluputhaanu
			I mixed	I am mixing	I will mix
68	aloochinchu	To think	aloochinchaanu	aloochisthunnaanu	aloochisthaanu
			I thought	I am thinking	I will think
69	ivvu	To give	ichaanu	isthunnaanu	isthaanu
			I gave	I am giving	I will give
70	pampu	To send	pampaanu	pamputhunnaanu	pamputhaanu
			I sent	I am sending	I will send
71	yekku	To climb	yekkaanu	yekkuthunnaanu	yekkuthaanu
			I climbed	I am climbing	I will climb
72	adugu	To ask	adigaanu	aduguthunnaanu	aduguthaanu
			I asked	I am asking	I will ask
73	nimpu	To fill	nimpaanu	nimputhunnaanu	nimputhaanu
			I filled	I am filling	I will fill
74	perugu	To grow	perigaanu	peruguthunnaanu	peruguthaanu
			I grew	I am growing	I will grow
75	yeeduvu	To cry	yeedichaanu	yeedusthunnaanu	yeedusthaanu
			I cried	I am crying	I will cry

LESSON 7: IMPERATIVE

Imperative: In Telugu, Imperative form of a verb is used to make requests, giving orders or simply asking someone to do something. Hence, there are two types of imperative:

1. Informal imperative (Similar to an order).

2. Polite or Formal Imperative (Similar to a request)

Informal Imperative: Informal Imperatives are used only for addressing someone younger than you, children's and servants. Please never use the Informal imperative form with elders or a person who is higher in position, as it will offend them and put you in a very embarrassing situation.

An Informal imperative is just the root form of a verb which you have already memorized.

For Example: You are a secretary for the general manager and yourself and your general manager are in a meeting and in the middle of the meeting he looks at you and says 'raayi' (write); it means that he is instructing you to write down what's being discussed in the meeting.

Example:

Telugu Verb	English (Like an Instruction)
laagu	Pull
cherupu	Erase
chimpu	Tear
thokku	Step on
gamaninchu	Observe
navvu	Laugh
kuttu	Stich

Polite or Formal Imperative: Formal Imperative is used when you are addressing a stranger, someone older than you, and someone who is higher in position. When you using the Formal

Imperative, the word 'Please' gets automatically added to your formal imperative; you don't have to use a separate word to say 'Please' here. Formal Imperative can be used to issue a command in a more polite way to one or more person (plural).

The suffix to make a verb root as Formal Imperative is '-andi':

Example:

chuudu (to see) + '-andi' = chuudandi (Please see)

kuurchu (to sit) + '-andi' = kuurchandi (Please sit)

ivvu (to give) + '-andi' = ivvandi (Please give)

thinu (to eat) + '-andi' = thinnandi (Please eat)

chadhuvu (to read) + '-andi' = chadhuvandi (Please read)

Note: As you saw in the above example, the word 'Please' get automatically added to the sentence. In Telugu, we hardly use a separate word for 'Please'; it is usually added in a sentence when you have a suffix which denotes formal or politeness.

Note: In Telugu, the word for 'Please' is 'dhayacheesi', but this is really extreme. We use 'dhayacheesi' very rarely and in a very extreme and desperate situation. For example, when you need to borrow some money from your friends or you need a huge favor from someone.

LESSON 8: NUMBERS AND TIME

Numbers:

Numbers in Telugu are almost similar to English with some variation.

From 1 to 19:

Number 1 to 19 is unique words so you will have to memorize them as it is.

Telugu	English	Telugu	English
okati	One	padhakondu	Eleven
rendu	Two	pannendu	Twelve
muudu	Three	padhamuudu	Thirteen
naalugu	Four	padhnaalugu	Fourteen
aidhu	Five	padhiheenu	Fifteen
aaru	Six	padhahaaru	Sixteen
yeedu	Seven	padhiheedu	Seventeen
yenimidhi	Eight	padhenimidhi	Eighteen
thommidhi	Nine	panthommidhi	Nineteen
padhi	Ten		

Note: When you are referring to the number 'one', then you should use 'okati'; rest of the time you should use 'okka' (’a’, ‘an’, ‘one’).

From 20 to 99:

Here, you have to memorize only the ten's form (e.g. twenty, thirty, forty etc.), Then the rest of them will follow as a pattern.

Telugu	English
iravai	Twenty
iravai okati	Twenty-one
iravai rendu	Twenty-two
mupphai	Thirty
mupphai okati	Thirty-one
nalabhai	Forty
nalabhai okati	Forty-one
yaabhai	Fifty
yaabhai okati	Fifty-one
aravai	Sixty
aravai okati	Sixty-one
debbhai	Seventy
debbhai okati	Seventy-one
yenabhai	Eighty
yenabhai okati	Eighty-one
thombhai	Ninety
thombhai okati	Ninety-one

As you see in the above table, I just added the number 'okati' next to the Twenty, Thirty, Forty and so on. All you have to do is memorize the ten's form and add "okati, rendu, muudu, naalugu and so on" next to it as per your requirement.

Sixty-Nine = aravai aaru

From 100 to 199:

Hundred = vandha

You will use 'vandha', only when you refer to 'Hundred'. Other than that, you will always use the word 'nuuta' when you want to form numbers from 100 to 199. Please refer to the below table for more examples.

Telugu	English
nuuta okati	Hundred and one
nuuta rendu	Hundred and two
nuuta muudu	Hundred and three
nuuta naalugu	Hundred and four
nuuta aidhu	Hundred and five
nuuta aaru	Hundred and six
nuuta yeedu	Hundred and seven
nuuta yenimidhi	Hundred and eight
nuuta thommidhi	Hundred and nine
nuuta padhi	Hundred and ten

Using the above you will be able to form 100 - 199 in Telugu all by yourself.

Example:

123 = nuuta iravai muudu

143 = nuuta nalabhai muudu

132 = nuuta mupphai rendu

162 = nuuta aravai rendu

179 = nuuta debbhai thommidhi

183 = nuuta yenabhai muudu

From 200 to 999:

You will always use the word 'vandhala' as a representation of 'Hundred and' when you want to form numbers from 200 to 999. Please refer to the below table for more examples.

Telugu	English
rendu vandhala okati	Two hundred and one
muudu vandhala rendu	Three hundred and two
naalugu vandhala muudu	Four hundred and three
aidhu vandhala naalugu	Five hundred and four
aaru vandhala aidhu	Six hundred and five
yeedu vandhala aaru	Seven hundred and six
yenimidhi vandhala yeedu	Eight hundred and seven
thommidhi vandhala yenimidhi	Nine hundred and eight

Using the above table, you will be able to form 200 - 999 in Telugu all by yourself.

Example:

223 = rendu vandhala iravai muudu

443 = naalugu vandhala nalabhai muudu

532 = aidhu vandhala mupphai rendu

762 = yeedu vandhala aravai rendu

879 = yenimidhi vandhala debbhai thommidhi

983 = thommidhi vandhala yenabhai muudu

Example:

223 = rendu vandhala iravai muudu

rendu - Two

vandhala - Hundred and

iravai - Twenty

muudu - Three

From 1,000 to 1,999:

Thousand = veyyi

You will use 'veyyi' only from 1000 - 1099. Other than that, you will always use the (11 -19) (padhakondu - panthommidhi) form when you want to form numbers from 1,100 to 1,999. Please refer to the below table for more examples.

	Telugu	English
1001	veyyi okati	Thousand and one
1011	veyyi padhakondu	Thousand and eleven
1120	padhakondu vandhala iravai	One thousand one hundred and twenty
1230	pannendu vandhala mupphai	One thousand two hundred and thirty
1300	padhamuudu vandhalu	One thousand three hundred
1449	padhnaalugu vandhala nalabhai thommidhi	One thousand four hundred and forty-nine
1550	padhiheenu vandhala yaabbhai	One thousand five hundred and fifty
1645	padhahaaru vandhala nalabhai aidhu	One thousand six hundred and forty-five
1732	padhiheedu vandhala mupphai rendu	One thousand seven hundred and thirty two
1890	padhenimidhi vandhala thombhai	One thousand eight hundred and ninety
1960	panthommidhi vandhala aravai	One thousand nine hundred and sixty

The above table might be a little confusing for you, as we use a different form in English, but to be honest this makes your life easier.

For example:

1969 - One thousand nine hundred and sixty-nine.

As you see in the above example, it is such a long form to simply say the number 1969 in English. That's the reason, in English for the year 1969 we simply say "nineteen sixty nine" rather than saying "One thousand nine hundred and sixty nine", which will be super annoying for us as we use the "years" a lot while we speak and every time we have to say the whole thing like a sentence itself.

That's why in Telugu we use 1969 - panthommidhi vandhala aravai thommidhi

panthommidhi - Nineteen

vandhala - Thousand and

aravai - Sixty

thommidhi - Nine

Also, you would have recognized from the above table that for '1300' I used 'padhamuudu vandhalu' instead of 'padhamuudu vandhala'. When you have additional number, you will use 'vandhala' otherwise you would use vandhalu. Please refer to the table below for more clarity on this.

	Telugu	**English**
1200	pannendu vandhalu	One thousand two hundred
1300	padhamuudu vandhalu	One thousand three hundred
1400	padhnaalugu vandhalu	One thousand four hundred
1500	padhiheenu vandhalu	One thousand five hundred
1600	padhahaaru vandhalu	One thousand six hundred
1700	padhiheedu vandhalu	One thousand seven hundred
1800	padhenimidhi vandhalu	One thousand eight hundred
1900	panthommidhi vandhalu	One thousand nine hundred

Other than the above situation, you would always use 'vandhala'.

From 2,000 to 99,999:

Two thousand = rendu vela

You will use 'vela' as a representation of 'thousand and' from 2000 - 99,999. Please refer to the table below for more examples.

	Telugu	**English**
2001	rendu vela okati	Two thousand and one
3011	muudu vela padhakondu	Three thousand and eleven
3120	muudu vela nuuta iravai	Three thousand one hundred and twenty
4230	naalugu vela rendu vandhala mupphai	Four thousand two hundred and thirty
5300	aidhu vela muudu vandhalu	Five thousand three hundred
6449	aaru vela naalugu vandhala nalabhai thommidhi	Six thousand four hundred and forty-nine
7550	yeedu vela aidhu vandhala yaabhai	Seven thousand five hundred and fifty
8645	yenimidhi vela aaru vandhala nalabhai aidhu	Eight thousand six hundred and forty-five
9732	thommidhi vela yeedu vandhala mupphai rendu	Nine thousand seven hundred and thirty-two
10890	padhi vela yenimidhi vandhala thombhai	Ten thousand eight hundred and ninety

10890 - padhi vela yenimidhi vandhala thombhai

padhi - Ten

vela - Thousand and

yenimidhi - Eight

vandhala - Hundred and

thombhai - ninety

Similar to the usage of 'vandhalu' and 'vandhala' we use 'velu' and 'vela'. When you have additional number, you will use 'vela' otherwise you would use 'velu'. Please refer to the below table for more clarity on this.

	Telugu	English
20000	iravai velu	Two thousand
30000	mupphai velu	Three thousand
40000	nalabhai velu	Four thousand
50000	yaabhai velu	Five thousand
60000	aravai velu	Six thousand
70000	debbhai velu	Seven thousand
80000	yenabhai velu	Eight thousand
90000	thombhai velu	Nine thousand

90,000 - thombhai velu: (thombhai - Ninety, velu - Thousand)

Lakhs and Crore:

In India, we use lakh's and crore's instead of using billions and millions.

a) laksha (a lakh) (one hundred thousand)

b) kooti (a crore) (ten million)

Note: 100 Lakhs = 1 Crore; 100 laksha = 1 kooti,

The same rule like the previous one applies here too, but it is more complicated for someone from America and other countries because Indian numbering system is different.

Example:

a) One Hundred thousand five hundred and five (100,505). (American number system)

One Lakh five hundred and five (1,00,505). (Indian number system)

oka kooti aidhu vandhala aidhu (1,00,505).

b) Eighteen million one hundred and fifty thousand (18,150,000). (American number system)

One crore and eighty-one lakhs and fifty thousand (1,81,50,000). (Indian number system)

oka kooti yenabhai oka lakshala yaabhai velu (1,81,50,000).

Ordinal Numbers in Telugu:

Ordinal numbers in Telugu are similar to -th (e.g. Fifth, Sixth) in English. To create an ordinal number in Telugu you should simply add the suffix -ava to the Telugu number.

Example:

Combination	Telugu	English
okati + ava	okatava	First
rendu + ava	rendava	Second
muudu + ava	muudava	Third
naalugu + ava	naalugava	Fourth
aidhu + ava	aidhava	Fifth
aaru (exception)	aravadhi / aaro	Sixth
yeedu + ava	yeedava	Seventh
yenimidhi + ava	yenimidhava	Eighth
thommidhi + ava	thommidhava	Ninth
padhi + ava	padhava	Tenth

First Class: (okati) (one) + (ava) (-st) + (tharagathi) (class) = okatava tharagathi (First Class)

Example:

Telugu	English
okatava viidhi	First street
rendava varusa	Second line
muudava roju	Third day
naalugava nela	Fourth month
aidhava tharagathi	Fifth class
aravadhi / aaro illu	Sixth house
yeedhava koduku	Seventh son

yenimidhava kuuthuru	Eighth daughter
thommidhava abbaayi	Ninth Boy
padhava ammaayi	Tenth girl
... and so on	

Telling the Time:

Telling the time in Telugu is similar to the way we say it in English.

Important Vocabulary for telling time: gantalu (hour, o'clock); nimishaalu (minutes);

Example:

a) yenimidhi gantalu (8 o'clock)

b) yenimidhi ayindhi (It is 8 o'clock)

c) mupphai yeedu nimishaalu (Thirty-seven minutes)

When you want to indicate 'at' a particular time, then you would use the dative case of 'ku' as 'gantaluku' (at time)) proceeded by the appropriate number.

Example:

a) yenimidhi gantaluku (At 8 o'clock)

b) yenimidhi gantaluku veldhaam (Let's go at 8 o'clock)

For every quarter of an hour the below mentioned suffixes are added to the numeral.

- -n + paav = 'quarter' (15 minutes)
- -n + ara = 'half' (30 minutes)
- -n + muppaav = 'three quarters' (45 minutes)

Example:

a) Time yentha? (Informal) (What is the time?), "Time yenthandi?" or Time yentha aiyindhi andi? (Formal) (What is the time, please?).

b) yenimidhin paav aiyindhi andi

lit/t: it's eight fifteen, It's quarter past eight

yenimidhi + -n + paav = yenimidhin paav

c) muudun ara aiyindhi andi

lit/t: it's three thirty, It's half past three

muudu + -n + ara = muudun ara

d) yenimidhin muppaav aiyindhi andi

lit/t: it's eight forty-five, It's quarter to nine.

yenimidhi + -n + muppaav = yenimidhin muppaav

e) yenimidhin paavku

lit/t: At eight fifteen, at quarter past eight

f) muudun araku

lit/t: At three thirty, at half past three

g) yenimidhin muppaavku

lit/t: At eight forty-five, at quarter to nine.

Exercises:

A) Write the following numbers in Telugu.

a) 36, b) 78, c) 269, d) 99, e) 966, f) 3689, g) 145, h)5987, i) 98,758, j) 6,98,750.

B) Tell the time; let's say that someone is asking you for the time every hour from 2 o'clock until 8.

Example: Time yentha?

   rendu ayindhi.

C) Tell the time by every quarter of an hour; let's say that someone is asking you the time every quarter of an hour from 2 o'clock until 4.

Example: Time yentha?

   rendu ayindhi.

   rendun paav ayindhi.

D) Translate the time given below in Telugu.

Example: 5.10

Answer: aidhu padhi

 a) 5.25, b) 6.36, c) 11.22, d) 9.27, e) 4.30.

Solutions

Exercise A

a) mupphai aaru b) debbhai yenimidhi c) rendu vandhala arava thommidhi d) thombhai thommidhi e) thommidhi vandhala aravai aaru f) muudu vela aaru vandhala yenabhai thommidhi g) nuuta nalabhai aidhu h) aidhu vela thommidhi vandhala yenabhai yeedu i) thombhai yenimidhi vela yeedu vandhala yaabhai yenimidhi j) aaru lakshala thombhai yenimidhi vela yeedu vandhala yaabhai.

Exercise B

1) rendu ayindhi 2) muudu ayindhi 3) naalugu ayindhi 4) aidhu ayindhi 5) aaru ayindhi 6) yeedu ayindhi 7) yenimidhi ayindhi.

Exercise C

1) rendun paav ayindhi 2) rendun ara ayindhi 3) rendun mupaav ayindhi 4) muudu ayindhi 5) muudun paav ayindhi 6) muudun ara ayindhi 7) muudun mupaav ayindhi 8) naalugu ayindhi.

Exercise D

1) aidhu iravai aidhu 2) aaru mupphai aaru 3) padhakondu iravai rendu 4) thommidhi iravai yeedu 5) naalugu mupphai

Asking for Directions:

When are asking for directions in Telugu, some people will give you directions in Telugu and some with replace some Telugu words with English words while giving you directions especially in the city.

Useful vocabulary while asking for directions:

Telugu	English
pakkaku, vaipu	Side
yedama pakkaku or yedama vaipu	Left
kudi pakkaku or kudi vaipu	Right
neeruga	Straight
venuka vaipuku / venukaku	Back, Back side
mundhu vaipuku / mundhuku	Front, Front side
viidhi	Street
veLLandi	Please go
thirugandi	Please turn

The below table provides you frequently provided directions:

	Telugu (Village and some places in city)	Telugu (City)	English
⬅	yedama pakkaku / vaipuku veLLandi or thirugandi	Left ki veLLandi	Please go Left side or Please turn Left side
➡	kudi pakkaku / vaipuku veLLandi or thirugandi	Right ki veLLandi	Please go Right side or Please turn Right side
⬆	neeruga veLLandi	straight ga veLLandi	Please go straight
⬇	mundhuku veLLandi	back ki veLLandi	Please go back side

Note: You can also use "thirugandi" instead of "veLLandi" except when you refer to going straight or front. (E.g. yedama pakkaku thirugandi (Please turn right), kudi pakkaku thirugandi (Please turn left).

Examples:

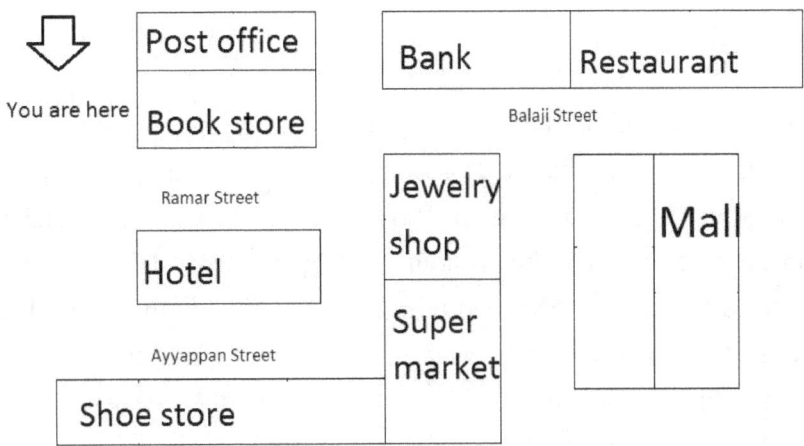

The below example is about asking a person 'how to go to the mall' and 'he is guiding you';

I have split the guiding into multiple sentence for easy understanding.

dhaani tharuvatha - after that

a) mallki yela veLLaali?

lit: to the mall how should go

t: How to go to the mall?

b) neeruga veLLandi, yedama pakkaku thirugandi, dhaani tharuvatha neeruga veLLandi

t: Go straight, Turn Left side, After that go straight

c) yedama pakkaku thirugandi, dhaani tharuvatha kudi pakkaku thirugandi, dhaani tharuvatha neeruga veLLandi

t: Turn left side, after that turn right side, after that go straight

d) kudi pakkaku thirugandi, dhaani tharuvatha neeruga veLLandi, mii kudi pakkaku Mall undeedhi.

lit: Turn right side, after that go straight, on your right-side Mall will be there.

LESSON 9: CASES

As discussed earlier, Case endings are added to nouns and pronouns, which will give them the ability to express grammatical relations (e.g. subject, direct object, possession etc.). Also, the prepositions that we use in English (e.g. 'in', 'to', 'for', 'from', etc.). In English usually we add these prepositions before a noun or the pronoun, for e.g. 'In the book', 'with him', 'to the office', 'for her' etc. Whereas in Telugu we will add these prepositions in the form of a suffix and add it to the word itself (like a word ending). These are called case endings.

For example, In English we use the suffix '-ist' to indicate 'the one who does', e.g. chemist, activist, alchemist, biologist etc. here we added the suffix '-ist' to each profession to point out the person who does it.

Important Note: You can add only one case suffix to a noun or a pronoun.

There are 8 case endings in Telugu, kindly find them in detail below.

1) Nominative Case: This is used in the subject of the sentence; this is a basic form of a noun or a pronoun and you don't have to add any suffix to it.

Example:

a) aayana paaduthunnaaru (He is singing) (polite)

b) aavida parigeduthunnaaru (She is running) (polite)

c) nenu thintunnaanu (I am eating)

d) nuvvu veLLaavu (You went) (impolite)

e) miiru aadukunnaaru (You played) (polite)

f) vaaLLu rasthaaru (They will write)

g) meemu kaduguthaamu (We will wash)

In the above examples, I didn't add any suffix to the subject of the sentence (aayana, aavida, nenu, nuvvu, miiru, vaaLLu, meemu) because it is a Nominative case, the basic form of the noun.

Note: Nominative Case is a basic form of the subject.

List of Nominative Pronouns:

	Singular	Plural
	Nominative	Nominative
First person	nenu (I)	manamu (we) (listener included)
		meemu (we) (listener not included)
Second person	nuvvu (you)	miiru (You) (Polite)
	miiru (You) (Polite)	
Third person	athanu/vaadu (he)	vaaLLu (they-human) (polite)
	aayana (he) (polite)	
	aame (she)	
	aavida (she) (polite)	
	adhi (that) idhi (this), both the word also means it.	avi (those) ivi (these)

Important Note: From here on, the remaining 5 cases will not use the Nominative case pronoun from the above table, they will use Cases form pronoun which will be provided in the respective cases as a table.

2) Accusative Suffix:
Accusative case is used in a direct object of the sentence. The suffix to be used in Accusative case are ("-ni (things, animals) and -nu (Human beings)"). But this suffix is optional, even if you don't use this suffix in a sentence containing the accusative case, it would still make sense but native Telugu speakers tend to use this suffix. Hence, I would recommend you not to be so concerned about the Accusative suffix when you forgot to use them. As long as you understand why a native speaker uses this suffix, everything is good.

What is a Direct Object?

A direct object is a noun or pronoun that receives the action of the verb directly, without any prepositions separating the verb from the receiver. The direct object answers the question "whom?" or "what?" in regards to the verb. A direct object always follows a Transitive verb in English; a direct object is always followed by a Transitive verb in Telugu because in Telugu the object of the sentence usually comes next to a verb whereas in English it's the opposite.

Direct object follows Transitive Verb: This means Direct object comes or happens after Transitive verb. Subject Verb Object (SVO).

Direct object is followed by Transitive Verb: This means Transitive Verb comes or happens after Direct object. Subject Object Verb (SOV).

The direct object in a sentence is always a noun. It may also be in the form of a noun such as a pronoun, noun clause or a noun phrase. However, a direct object will always function as a noun.

What is a Transitive Verb?

Verbs that take a direct object are called Transitive verbs; these verbs are always followed by a noun or pronoun.

Example in English:

a. Ram kicked the ball.

- In the above sentence, it answers the question 'what is Ram kicking?'
- What is the direct object in this sentence? The direct object in this sentence is 'Ball' because the noun 'Ball' is the one which answers the question 'what'.
- What is the Transitive verb in this sentence? The Transitive verb in this sentence is 'kicked' because it takes the direct object 'Ball' next to it.

Example in Telugu: Vocabulary: banthi (Ball).

b) Ram banthini thannaadu.

lit: Ram the ball kicked.

t: Ram kicked the ball.

In detail: banthi (Ball) + '-ni' (Accusative suffix) = banthini (The ball)

- In the above sentence, it answers the question 'ram dhenini thannaadu?'.
  lit: Ram what did kicked.

  t: What did Ram kicked.

- What is the direct object in this sentence? The direct object in this sentence is 'banthini' (Ball) because the noun 'banthini' is the one which answers the question 'dhenni' (what).

- What is the Transitive verb in this sentence? The Transitive verb in this sentence is 'thannaadu' because it takes the direct object 'banthini' before it.

How to Find the Direct Object in a Sentence in Telugu?

A simple formula given below can help you identify a direct object in a sentence.

Formula:

- Subject + What? or Whom? + Action Verb.

- What? or Whom? = Direct Object.

Example of Direct Object Sentence Formula:

- (Lakshmi) (name of a girl) (subject) + (pusthakamni) (book) (what? or whom?) + (thiiskunnaaru) (took) (action verb) (polite).

- pusthakamni = direct object.

- **In detail**: (pusthakam) (book) + '-ni' (Accusative suffix) = pusthakamni.

We could also say "Lakshmi pusthakamu thiiskunnaaru". As mentioned earlier, the suffix 'ni/nu' is optional. Even if you don't use them the sentence would still make sense but it is common that the native speakers use this suffix while making a sentence which has an accusative case.

- nenu illu konnaanu (I bought a house)

- nenu kukkani konnaanu (I bought a dog)

- nenu bus yekkaanu (I boarded a bus)

Important Note: As per the above examples, it should be clear on "What is an accusative suffix in Telugu and how to use the suffix 'ni'. As mentioned in the beginning, we use the accusative suffix '-ni' when we refer to an animal or a thing as a direct object and we will use the accusative suffix '-nu' when we refer to a human being as a direct object. Please refer to the below example and table for more clarity on this.

Example in English:

a. Please call them.

- In the above sentence, it answers the question 'Whom should I call?'
- What is the direct object in this sentence? The direct object in this sentence is 'them' because the pronoun 'them' is the one which answers the question 'whom'.
- What is the Transitive verb in this sentence? The Transitive verb in this sentence is 'call' because it takes the direct object 'them' next to it.

Example in Telugu:

b) vaaLLanu pillavandi

lit: them please call

t: Please call them.

In detail: vaaLLu (Them) + '-nu' (Accusative suffix) = vaaLLanu (Them)

Important Note: In accusative cases and in all other case form except nominative case, the pronoun vaLLu becomes vaLLa.

- What is the direct object in this sentence? The direct object in this sentence is 'vaaLLanu' (Them).
- What is the Transitive verb in this sentence? The Transitive verb in this sentence is 'pilavandi' because it takes the direct object 'vaaLLunu' before it.

How to Find the Direct Object in a Sentence in Telugu?

A simple formula given below can help you identify a direct object in a sentence.

Formula:

- Subject + What? or Whom? + Action Verb.
- What? or Whom? = Direct Object.

Example of Direct Object Sentence Formula:

- (Ram) (name of a man) (subject) + (ravananu) (name of a man) (whom?) + (champaaru) (killed) (action verb) (polite).
- ravananu = direct object.
- **In detail**: (ravana) (name of a man) + -nu (Accusative suffix) = ravananu.

Note: There are pros and cons in the accusative case. **Cons:** Accusative case will be difficult for native English speakers because we don't have them in English. **Pros:** Even if you don't use the Accusative suffix in a sentence with accusative case, it would sound little odd for the native Telegu speakers but the sentence would still make sense and its correct.

3) Dative Case: Dative case suffix refers to the preposition 'For'. Dative case is used in a sentence when it is referring to "giving 'for' someone/something". The suffix to be used in Dative case are '-ku/ki' and 'kosam'.

Usage:

Usage in English	Usage in Telugu
In English, we usually use the preposition 'for' when we want to do something for another person or an object. It can be a favour or a necessity, but it clearly indicated that we are doing this only for that particular person or an object. **Example:** I came for you.	It's the same in Telugu as well. We use the Telugu word 'kosam' (for) for this purpose. **Example:** nenu nii kosam vochchaanu lit: I for you came t: I came for you.
In English, when we want something, we use the word 'want'. The English word 'want' clear indicates that you desire it, it can be an object or an activity etc. **Example:** I want chocolate.	In Telugu, the word for want is 'kavaali'. Similar to English the word 'kavaali' clearly indicates that you desire it or desire to do that activity etc. But, In Telugu, adding to this we should also use the suffix '-ku/ki' next to the pronoun/subject of the sentence. This clearly indicates "who desires it". Here "ku/ki" represents the word 'for'. The below example will make it much clearer for you. **Example:** naaku chocolate kavaali lit: for me chocolate want t: I want chocolate / for me want chocolate **In Detail:** naaku (for me), kavaali (want)

With the above explanation, I think I made it clear that "In Telugu, we specifically point out who is desiring it".

116

English	Telugu
I want	For me want
Peter want	For peter want
Bank wants	For bank wants

The below table provides the list of pronouns with their respective Dative case 'kosam'.

Pronoun	Suffix	Dative pronoun	English
naa	kosam	naa kosam	For me.
nii	kosam	nii kosam	For you (Informal).
mii	kosam	mii kosam	For you (Formal).
athani	kosam	athani kosam	For him (Informal).
aayana	kosam	aayana kosam	For him (Formal).
aame	kosam	aame kosam	For her (Informal).
aavida	kosam	aavida kosam	For her (Formal).
dhaani	kosam	dhaani kosam	For that (it)
dhiini	kosam	dhiini kosam	For this (it)
maa	kosam	maa kosam	For us (Inclusive)
mana	kosam	mana kosam	For us (Exclusive)
viiti	kosam	viiti kosam	For those
vaati	kosam	vaati kosam	For these
vaaLLa	kosam	vaaLLa kosam	For them

The below table provides the list of pronouns with their respective Dative case 'ku/ki'.

Pronoun	Suffix	Dative pronoun	English
naa	ku	naaku	For me.
nii	ku	niiku	For you (Informal).
mii	ku	miiku	For you (Formal).
athani	ki	athaniki	For him (Informal).
aayana	ki	aayanaki	For him (Formal).
aame	ki	aameki	For her (Informal).
aavida	ki	aavidaki	For her (Formal).
dhaani	ki	dhaaniki	For that (it)
dhiini	ki	dhiiniki	For this (it)
maa	ku	maaku	For us (Inclusive)
mana	ku	manaku	For us (Exclusive)
viiti	ki	viitiki	For those
vaati	ki	vaatiki	For these
vaaLLa	ku	vaaLLaku	For them

As mentioned earlier, usually you would use the suffix 'ku/ki', when the sentence contains the word 'want' in Telugu. But there are few other situations where we would use this suffix; since they are very few, I am not going to explain them now.

In the above table you would have recognized that I used the dative suffix '-ku' for some pronouns and the suffix '-ki' for some pronouns. If you ask me 'why do we use the suffix '-ku' for some pronoun and '-ki' for some pronouns' I don't have a clear explanation for that. Maybe it's for easy pronunciation. Since, it's a small rule I would just recommend you to memorize them and use it as it is.

Dative case is used in the word which is on the receiving end. Dative case may also be used in front of some conjugated verbs. Basically, Dative case is used in Noun, Pronoun and Verbs.

Example:

a) India + kosam = India kosam (for India).

b) America + kosam = America kosam (for America).

c) akka (elder sister + kosam = akka kosam (for elder sister).

d) i pen akka kosam.

lit/t: This pen is for elder sister.

Note: In the above example we are using akka kosam (for elder sister) instead of akka (elder sister) because the 'elder sister' is at the receiving end, she is the one who is receiving the pen. Also, this sentence answers the question 'This pen is for whom?'.

e) nenu maa amma kosam Ice cream chesaanu.

lit: I for my mom ice cream made.

t: I made ice cream for my mom.

f) nenu vegetables konadam kosam market ki veLthunnaanu

lit: I for buying vegetables to the market going

t: I am going to the market for buying vegetables.

g) naaku coffee kavaali

lit: for me coffee want

t: I want coffee

h) miiku pizza kavaali

lit: for you pizza want

t: You want pizza

i) miiku pizza kavaalaa?

lit: for you pizza want?

t: Do you want pizza?

j) peterki pizza kavaalaa?

lit: for peter pizza want?

t: Does peter want pizza?

Usage of "Want" in Telugu

In Telugu, we precisely use the word 'want'. So, unlike English, where we use the word 'want' in many situations. Whereas in Telugu the words and form will change depending on what you are pointing to.

We use the suffix "-aali" to indicate "have to/must/should"

Example:

a) thinu (to eat) + -aali = thinaali (must eat / should eat / have to eat)

b) cheyyi (to do) + -aali = cheyyaaali (must do / should do / have to do)

c) nuvvu raayi (to write) + -aali = nuvvu raayaaali (you must write / you should write / you have to write)

d) athanu paadu (to sing) + -aali = athanu paadaaali (he must sing / he should sing / he has to sing)

Note: As mentioned earlier, whenever you add a suffix to a word and the word ends with the letter 'u' or 'i' or 'o', then the last letter will be removed then a suffix is being added to it.

With the above concept clear, now we will see "how to use the other form of 'want'".

Example: Vocabulary: ani = desire, undhi = is there.

a) naaku thinaali ani undhi

lit: for me should eat desire is there.

t: I want to eat.

If the above example scares you, then I understand why. But this is an exceptional case. In Telugu, we shouldn't simply say that we want to do, instead we should say that we have the desire to perform that activity and this is applicable only for performing an activity. Whenever you want to perform an activity then you should use this form. There is no other choice and this form is fixed so you just have to memorize them and use it like a thumb rule. Initially, it would be difficult for you but after making few practice sentences you will be able to form such statements easily. Like I mentioned earlier, just accept them as it is and practice the form, and you will be able to use them naturally in no time.

b) athaniki paadaali ani undhi

lit: for him should sing desire is there.

t: He wants to sing.

c) vaallaku raayaali ani undhi

lit: for then should write desire is there.

t: They want to write.

d) manaku veLLaali ani undhi

lit: for us should go desire is there.

t: We want to go.

Now, to summarize the different usage of want in Telugu.

1. naaku cake kavaali (I want chocolate) (lit: for me want chocolate)

As per the above sentence, you will use the word 'kavaali' when you want something.

2. naaku cake thinaali ani undhi (I want to eat cake) (lit: for me cake have to eat desire is there)

As per the above sentence, you will use the words 'ani undhi' (desire is there) when you want to perform an action.

Exercise:

A) Use Dative suffix to translate the following from English to Telugu.

e.g. My elder sister wants coffee

Answer: naa akka ki coffee kavaali

1) My younger brother wants tea.

2) I want to go to the shop.

3) This computer is for my father

4) That book is for my elder brother.

5) I want to eat.

6) She wants to cook.

7) I want to eat this pesarattu tomorrow

8) They want a statue.

9) I want to go to the mall today.

10) I want to eat here.

4) Genitive/Possessive Case: Genitive case suffix refers to the preposition 'of', "'s'. Genitive case is used to indicate Possession. The suffix to be used in Genitive case is -yokka for possessive adjective and the suffix '-dhi' for possessive pronoun.

The Genitive case suffix for possessive adjective is optional for both nouns and pronouns, but you should use only the case form pronouns not the Nominative pronouns. The Genitive case suffix is mostly omitted with pronouns than with nouns. So, you will find lots of nouns containing this suffix but very rarely you will find a pronoun with this suffix but you should still learn this so that you can recognize it when required. This suffix is used when the sentence answers the question 'whose', then the answer would be 'of ....' , '.....'s'.

The below table provides the list of pronoun with their respective Genitive case.

Pronoun with Genitive Suffix	Pronoun without Genitive Suffix	English	Genitive (possessive pronoun)	English
naa yokka	naa	My	naadhi	Mine
nii yokka	nii	Your (Informal).	niidhi	Yours (Informal).
mii yokka	mii	Your (Formal).	miidhi	Yours (Formal).
athani yokka	athani	His (Informal).	athanidhi	His (Informal).
aayana yokka	aayana	His (Formal).	aayanadhi	His (Formal).
aame yokka	aame	Her (Informal).	aamedhi	Her's (Informal).
aavida yokka	aavida	Her (Formal), Their	aavidadhi	Her's, Theirs
dhaani yokka	dhaani	it's	dhaanidhi	it's
dhiini yokka	dhiini	it's	dhiinidhi	it's
maa yokka	maa	Our (Inclusive)	maadhi	Ours (Inclusive)
mana yokka	mana	Our (Exclusive)	manadhi	Ours (Exclusive)
vaati / viiti yokka	vaati / viiti	These / Those	vaatidhi/ viitidhi	These / Those
vaaLLa yokka	vaalla	Their	vaaLLadhi	Theirs

Example:

a) naa pusthakam

naa yokka pusthakam

lit/t: My Book.

Note: As mentioned earlier, the Genitive case for possessive adjective suffix is optional for both nouns and pronouns; hence you can use both the above-mentioned sentences with or without a suffix and it would still give you the same meaning. Both sentences above means 'My book'. Here I am stating that the 'book belongs to me' and 'I am in possession of the book'.

b) i pusthakam naadhi

lit/t: This book is mine

Note: As mentioned earlier, the above example is for Genitive case for possessive pronoun. The suffix '-dhi' for Genitive case for possessive adjective is mandatory otherwise if it is similar to English, then it wouldn't make any sense.

c) mana / mana yokka koththa car eruppu rangu

lit/t: Our new vehicle is red.

- mana / mana yokka = Pronoun in Genitive Case.
- car = Noun Receiving Possession.

d) a car niidhi

lit/t: That car is yours

e) idhi mii / mii yokka pillu

lit/t: This is your cat.

- mii / mii yokka = Pronoun in Genitive Case.
- pillu = Noun Receiving Possession.

f) i pillu vaalladhi

lit/t: This cat is theirs

g) idhi a phone / phone yokka sim card

lit/t: This is that phone's simcard.

h) i simcard a phonedhi

lit/t: That phones sim card

i) yedhi aame / aame yokka pusthakam?

lit/t: Which is her book?

Exercise:

B) Use Genitive suffix to translate the following from English to Telugu.

E.g. This is your Dog

Answer: idhi mii kukka

1) Is this your dog?

2) Whose cat is this?

3) This is your food

4) This is his home.

5) Is this her book?

6) Whose car is that?

7) She is his wife (Hint: With respect)

8) She is my wife. (Hint: With respect)

9) He is my husband. (Hint: With respect)

10) Is he your husband? (Hint: With respect)

11) This dog is mine

12) That car is yours

13) He is mine (He belongs to me)

14) Those flowers are hers.

15) This pencil is his.

5) Sociative Case: Sociative case suffix refers to the preposition 'along with'. Sociative case is used to indicate the person, animal or an object along with 'whom/that' the action was performed. To put it simply, Sociative case is used when you are socializing and it is not restricted to just a person. It also includes animals and objects, for e.g., you along with your friend or family, spoon along with fork, simcard along with phone etc. The suffix to be used in Instrumental case is -tho and naadheggara (nearby). Kindly find below details on when to use which suffix.

1) -tho - This Sociative suffix can be used for all.

2) -dheggara - nearby

Case pronoun	Pronoun with Instrumental Suffix	English
naa	naa tho	Along with me.
nii	nii tho	Along with you.
mii	mii tho	Along with you (Formal).
athani	athani tho	Along with him (Informal).
aayana	aayana tho	Along with him (Formal).
aame	aame tho	Along with her (Informal).
aavida	aavida tho	Along with her (formal).
dhaani	dhaani tho	Along with that (it)
dhiini	dhiini tho	Along with this (it)
maa	maa tho	Along with us (Inclusive)
mana	mana tho	Along with us (Exclusive)
vaati / viiti	vaati / viiti tho	Along with those / these
vaaLLa	vaaLLa tho	Along with them

Examples:

a) athani tho nenu party ki veLLaanu.

lit: along with him I to the party went.

t: I went to the party along with him.

- athani tho = Pronoun in Sociative Case.

- nenu = Pronoun Receiving social aspect.

b) nenu aame tho aadukunnaanu.

lit: I along with her was playing.

t: I was playing along with her.

c) pusthakam tho pen undhi

lit: along with the book, pen is there.

t: The pen is along with the book (Alternate: The pen was next to the book).

- pusthakam = Pronoun in Sociative Case.

- pen = Noun which simply indicates it was next to another object.

or

c) pusthakam dheggara pen undhi

lit: nearby to the book, pen is there.

t: The pen is nearby the book (Alternatively: The pen was next to the book).

- pusthakam = Pronoun in Sociative Case.

- pen = Noun which simply indicates it was next to another object.

d) phone tho simcard undeedhi.

lit: along with the phone simcard was there.

t: The simcard was there along with the phone.

or

d) phone dheggara simcard undeedhi.

lit: nearby to the phone simcard was there.

t: The simcard was nearby to the phone.

e) nenu naa amma tho unnaanu

lit: I along with my mother was there.

t: I was there with my mom.

- amma tho = Pronoun in Sociative Case.

- nenu = Pronoun Receiving social aspect.

f) aame naa chelli tho chadhivindhi

lit: she along with my younger sister studied.

t: She studied along with my younger sister.

g) idhi vaaLLa tho vochchindhi.

lit: it along with them came.

t: It came along with them.

- vaaLLa tho = Pronoun in Sociative Case.

Exercise:

C) Use Sociative suffix to translate the following from English to Telugu.

e.g. I will come to your house tomorrow with ram

Answer: nenu ram tho repu mii illu ki vochchusthaanu

lit: I along with ram tomorrow to your house will come.

t: I will come to your house tomorrow with ram

1) I ate my breakfast with my wife.

2) I went shopping along with my husband.

3) I was with my friends yesterday.

4) The book was along with the pencil.

5) I will sit with my friend, Maala.

6) Ablative Case: Ablative case suffix refers to the preposition 'from'. Ablative case indicates from where or from whom you got something, for e.g. I got the pen from him, the bulb got electricity from the generator etc. It is used to indicate both person and things.

The suffix to be used in Ablative case is "-nunchi". This suffix answers the question "from where".

Examples:

a) vaaLLu shop nunchi vochchaaru

lit: they from the shop came.

t: They came from the shop.

- shop nunchi = Noun in Ablative Case.

- vaaLLu = Pronoun which is from the location.

b) nenu America nunchi vochchaanu

lit: I from America am coming.

t: I am coming from America.

- America nunchi = Place in Ablative Case.

- nenu = Pronoun which is from the location.

c) aayana aavida nunchi pen thiiskunnaaru

lit: He from her pen took.

t: He took pen from her.

- aavida nunchi = Pronoun in Ablative Case.

- aayana = Pronoun which received.

d) nuvvu yevaru nunchi i car konnaavu

lit: you from whom this car bought.

t: From whom did you buy this car?

- yevaru nunchi = Question word in Ablative Case.

- Car= Noun which is being received.

Note: You can use Ablative case even with question words, like given in the above example.

e) nenu aayana nunchi i car konnaanu

lit: I from him this car bought.

t: I bought this car from him.

f) nenu aayana nunchi thiiskunnaanu

lit: I from him took.

t: I took from him.

g) aayana bank nunchi dabbu thiiskunnaaru

lit: he from the bank money took.

t: He took the money from the bank.

Exercises:

D) Try Responding to question 'From where do you come?' for the below mentioned 'using Ablative suffix'.

Example:

I; India.

Answer: nenu India nunchi vochchaanu. (I am coming from India)

1) I; Canada. 2) I; Srilanka. 3) I; Hotel. 4) I; House. 5) I; Shop.

E) Try Responding to question 'from whom did you take this ....?' for the below mentioned 'using Ablative suffix'.

Example:

Her; Money.

Answer: nenu aavida nunchi dabbu thiiskunnaanu (I took the money from her)

1) Him; Jewels; 2) Them; Car; 3) You (Formal); Book; 4) You (Informal Formal); Pencil; 5) Her; House.

F) Use Ablative suffix to translate the following from English to Telugu.

E.g. He took phone from me

Answer: aayana naa nunchi phone thiiskunnaaru

1) I got a letter from my friend.

2) She came from Hyderabad.

3) He is in the meeting from the morning.

4) I am coming from London

5) I bought this book from the shop

Other Ablative Suffixes: There are Three more suffixes associated with the Ablative case. These suffixes are not commonly used but if you know them, then you would be able to make much more sentences in Telugu. So, learn them but don't give too much importance to them.

1) The second suffix of Ablative case refers to the preposition 'valana' (because of). 'valana' (because of) indicates "for what reason an action took place".

Examples:

a) varsham valana nenu office ki veLLaledhu

lit: because of the rain, I to the office didn't go

t: I didn't go to the office because of the rain.

(varsham valana - because of the rain; veLLaledhu - didn't go)

b) sale valana shop crowded ga undhi

lit: because of the sale, the shop is crowded

t: The shop is crowded because of the sale

sale valana - because of the sale

c) aayana valana nenu kindhaku paddaanu

lit: because of him I fell down.

t: I fell down because of him.

2) The third suffix of Ablative case refers to the preposition 'kante' (than). 'kante (that) performs comparison between two things or two groups, or any animated or inanimated objects.

Examples

1. He is elder than me (athanu naa **kante** pedhdha vaadu)
2. This house is smaller than that (i illu dhaani **kante** chinnadhi)

3) The fourth suffix of Ablative case refers to the preposition 'batti' (according to).

Examples

1. I live according to my principles (nenu naa principles ni batti brathukuthaanu)
2. According to his report, there are 100 people. (athani report ni batti vandha mandhi unnaaru) (vandha mandhi - hundred people)

Other important Telugu prepositions

In this Lesson, you have already learnt most of the commonly used suffixes in their case forms. But there are many other suffixes which you can find in the below table, some of them are frequently used and some of them are rarely used. But if you learn them you will be able to build more sentences in Telugu and have good conversation with native Telugu speakers.

The below table provides the 21 Telugu prepositions with examples.

lt: Literally - I have provided literal translation for the sentences for better understanding.

	English	Telugu	Examples
1	To	ki	a) I am going to Hyderabad. (nenu Hyderabad ki veLthunnaanu) lit: I to the Hyderabad am going b) I am on the way to the station. (nenu station ki veLthunnaanu) lit: I to the station on the way
2	In	lo	a) I am in chennai (nenu chennai lo unnaanu) lit: I in Chennai am there b) The pen is in the drawer (drawer lo pen undhi) lit: in the drawer pen is there
3	Inside	lopala	a) Please come inside (lopalaki randi) lit: Inside please come b) The bird is inside the cage. (panjaram lopala pakshi undhi) lit: cage inside bird is there
4	Outside	bayata	a) Come out (bayataku randi) lit: outside please come b) The bird is outside the cage. (panjaran bayata pakshi undhi) lit: cage outside bird is there

5	About	gurinchi	I talked about the plan (nenu plan gurinchi matlaadaanu) lit: I Plan about talked
6	Till	varaku	I walked from here till there (nenu ikkada nunchi akkada varaku nadichaanu) lit: I here from there till walked
7	without	lekunda	I will not go without you(nuvvu lekunda nenu veLlalenu) lit: you without I will not go
8	near	dhaggara	I am near the park (nenu park dhaggara unnaanu) lit: I park near am there
9	on	miida	The cat is on the table (pilli balla miida undhi) lit: cat table on is there
10	After, Next	tharuvatha	a) January is after December (December tharuvatha January) lit: December after January b) After I come to Hyderabad, I will meet you. (nenu Hyderabad vochchina tharuvatha ninnu kalusthaanu.) lit: I Hyderabad come after you meet **Note:** the verb before the preposition 'tharuvatha' should contain a suffix 'ina'. c) After I eat the food, I will drink coffee. (nenu bhojanam chesina tharuvatha coffee thaaguthaanu) lit: I food do after coffee will drink d) I will go next year (nenu tharuvatha samvatsaram veLthaanu) lit: I next year will go
11	Before	mundhu	September is before October (October mundhu September) lit: October before September
12	up	paina	Please come up (painaku randi) lit: up please come

13	Down	kindha	Please come down (kindhaku randi) lit: down please come
14	Bottom	aduguna	The book is at the bottom (pusthakamu aduguna undhi) lit: book bottom is there
15	in front	mundhu	I am in front of the hospital (nenu hospital mundhu unnaanu) lit: I hospital in front am there
16	Last/Previous	poyina	I came from USA last year (nenu USA nunchi poyina samvatsaram vochchaanu lit: I USA from last year came
17	At (For location)	dhaggara	I will wait at the park (nenu park dhaggara wait chesthaanu) lit: I Park at wait will do
18	At (For time)	ku	I will come at 10 o'clock. (nenu padhi gantala ku vosthaanu) lit: I 10 o'clock at will come
19	Beside	pakkana	I sat beside you (nenu nii pakkana koorchunnaanu) lit: I your side sat
20	in the middle of	madhyalo	My house is in between mall and hospital. (maa illu mall ki hospital ki madhyalo undhi) lit: my house mall to hospital to in between is there.
21	through	dwaara	Train went through the channel. (Train channel dwaara veLLindhi.) lit: Train channel through went

Exercises:

G) Match the following Cases in the first column with the appropriate case suffixes in the second column.

1	Nominative	a	'ni/nu'
2	Accusative	b	yokka (optional)
3	Dative	c	'ku/ki', 'kosam'
4	Genitive	d	'nunchi', 'valana', 'kante', 'batti'
5	Sociative	e	-
6	Ablative	f	'tho', 'dheggara'

H) Choose the correct answer by choosing the right pronoun/object with case endings.

e.g. _____ chocolate kavaali.

a.nenu   b.naaku   c.naadhi

The correct answer is: 'naaku' chocolate kavaali (I want chocolate), since we use the word 'kavaali' (want) which belongs to the Dative case, we should use the dative case suffix 'ku/ki'. Hence, the correct answer is 'naaku'.

1. nenu _____ pillini thiiskunnaanu. (I took the cat from him)

a. athani nunchi   b. nunchi athani   c. athanini nunchi

2. _____ okka kukkani konnaanu. (I bought a dog)

a. nenu   b. naaku   c. nannu

3. _____ bandhi lo unnaaru. (They are in the vehicle)

a. aame   b. nannu   c. vaLLu

4. aame _____ bhojanam chesindhi. (She ate lunch with him)

a. athani tho   b. aame tho   c. yevaritho

5. nenu _____ paatashalaku veLLaanu. (I went to the school with him)

a. yevaritho   b. athani tho   c. aame tho

6. _____ nenu a shop ki veLLaanu. (I went to that shop because of them)

a. naa valana   b. athani valana   c. vaaLLa valana

7. _____ a shop ki veLLaaru. (They went to that shop)

a. athanu   b. vaaLLu   c. aame

8. _____ nenu a shop ki veLLaanu. (I went to that shop with them)

a. athani tho   b. vaaLLa tho   c. yevari tho

9. _____ i nela paniki veLLaanu. (I went to work this month)

a. athanu   b. nenu   c.adhi

10. nenu naa bhaarya _____ bhojanam thiiskochaanu. (I bought food for my wife)

a. ki   b. ku   c. ke

11. _____ thalupu vesaaru. (They closed the door)

a. yevaru   b. vaadu   c. vaaLLu

12. vaallu _____chadhivaaru. (They read the letter)

a. letternu   b. letter   c. letterku

13. nenu vaalla shop _____ thiiskochaanu. (I bought from their shop)

a. pakkana   b. nunchi   c. ki

14. nenu _____ thiikochaanu. (I took from them)

a. yevari nunchi   b. vaaLLa nunchi   c. aame nunchi

15. nuvvu _____ raavaali. (You must come here)

a. ikkadiki   b. akkadiki   c. yekkadiki

I) Translate the following sentences from English to Telugu using appropriate pronouns and objects with case endings and in nominative form.

E.g. He took phone from me

Answer: aayana naa nunchi phone thiiskunnaaru

1) He sat in the chair.

2) There is some milk in the fridge.

3) She was hiding under the table.

4) The cat jumped from the counter.

5) He drove on the bridge.

6) She lost her ring at the beach.

7) The book belongs to Anthony.

8) They were sitting beside the tree.

9) We are running in the gym today.

10) The sun is above the clouds.

11) She lives near her office.

12) He swam in the lake.

13) I walked in the street.

14) The car went through the tunnel.

15) I got a package from a friend.

16) She put the flowers beside/by the window.

17) The food was placed on the table.

18) I will get to the conference on time.

19) The baseball game was cancelled after the heavy rain.

20) John forgot his homework under the bed.

21) He succeeded with a little help.

22) I met him morning at 5am in the park

List of Pronouns for Different Cases

The below tables provide a list of case form Pronoun for all 5 cases except nominative.

Case form pronoun	Accusative	Dative	Dative (want)
-----	-ni/nu (optional)	-kosam	-ku/ki
naa	naanu	naa kosam	naaku
nii	niinu	nii kosam	niiku
mii	miinu	mii kosam	miiku
athani	athaninu	athani kosam	athaniki
aayana	aayananu	aayana kosam	aayanaki
aame	aamenu	aame kosam	aameki
aavida	aavidanu	aavida kosam	aavidaki
dhaani	dhaaninu	dhaani kosam	dhaaniki
dhiini	dhiininu	dhiini kosam	dhiiniki
maa	maanu	maa kosam	maaku
mana	mananu	mana kosam	manaku
viiti	viitinu	viiti kosam	viitiki
vaati	vaatinu	vaati kosam	vaatiki
vaaLLa	vaaLLanu	vaaLLa kosam	vaaLLaku

Genitive (possessive adjective)	Genitive (possessive pronoun)	Sociative	Ablative	Other Ablative forms
-yooka (optional)	-dhi	-tho	-nunchi	-valana/kante/batti
naa yokka	naadhi	naa tho	naa nunchi	naa valana/kante/batti
nii yokka	niidhi	nii tho	nii nunchi	nii valana/kante/batti
mii yokka	miidhi	mii tho	mii nunchi	mii valana/kante/batti
athani yokka	athanidhi	athani tho	athani nunchi	athani valana/kante/batti
aayana yokka	aayanadhi	aayana tho	aayana nunchi	aayana valana/kante/batti
aame yokka	aamedhi	aame tho	aame nunchi	aame valana/kante/batti
aavida yokka	aavidadhi	aavida tho	aavida nunchi	aavida valana/kante/batti
dhaani yokka	dhaanidhi	dhaani tho	dhaani nunchi	dhaani valana/kante/batti
dhiini yokka	dhiinidhi	dhiini tho	dhiini nunchi	dhiini valana/kante/batti
maa yokka	maadhi	maa tho	maa nunchi	maa valana/kante/batti
mana yokka	manadhi	mana tho	mana nunchi	mana valana/kante/batti
vaati / viiti yokka	vaatidhi/ viitidhi	vaati / viiti tho	vaati / viiti nunchi	vaati / viiti valana/kante/batti
vaaLLa yokka	vaaLLadhi	vaaLLa tho	vaaLLa nunchi	vaaLLa valana/kante/batti

Note: Case form pronoun is the base pronoun from which you add the case suffix endings; you should not confuse this with nominative pronouns (e.g. nenu)

FYI: In Telugu, we use lots of suffixes, but these 5 case suffixes (Accusative, Dative, Genitive, Sociative, Ablative) are the most important and the frequently used ones. You will find this suffix in most of the sentences; you can even form many sentences with just these suffixes.

Short Summary of Cases:

Case	Summary
Accusative:	The suffix is '-ni/nu' (optional). This suffix is used when the sentence answers the question of 'what' and 'whom', the answer would be 'is ...'.
Dative:	1. Same as the preposition 'for' in English. The suffix is '-kosam'. This suffix is used when the sentence answers the question 'for whom', the answer would be 'for ...'. 2. Whenever there is a sentence in Telugu with want, you should add the Dative suffix 'ku/ki' with the subject of the sentence. It also represents "for whom". In English we don't say this precisely but in Telugu we do.
Genitive:	1. possessive adjective: Same as the preposition 'of' "s" in English. The suffix is '-yokka'. This suffix is used when the sentence answers the question 'whose' and the answer would be 'of ....', '....'s'. 2. possessive pronoun: Same situation as the above but you won't have any noun next to the pronoun here. Same like in English. The suffix is '-dhi'. E.g. 'naa' or 'naa yokka' = my, 'naadhi' = mine.
Sociative:	Same as the preposition 'along with' in English. The suffix is '-tho'. This suffix is used when the sentence answers the question 'whom did you go with'.
Ablative:	1. Same as the preposition "from" in English. The suffix is '-nunchi'. This suffix answers the question "from where, from whom". 2. Same as the preposition "because of" in English. The suffix is '-valana'. This suffix answers the question "because of what/whom". 3. Same as the preposition "than" in English. The suffix is '-kante'. This suffix is use when you are comparing something. 4. The suffix is -batti. This suffix is used when you refer to something (according to whom/which).

Example: pusthakam (book)

Case	With case ending	English
Nominative	pusthakam	Book
Accusative	pusthakani or pusthakam	The Book
Dative	pusthakam kosam / pusthakam ki	For the book
Genitive	pusthakam yokka or pusthakam	Book's
Genitive	pusthakamdhi (possessive pronoun)	Book's
Sociative	pusthakam tho or pusthakam dheggara	Along with the book or near the book
Ablative	pusthakam nunchi, pusthakam valana, pusthakam kante, pusthakam batti	From the book, Because of the book, than the book, According to the book.

Example: aayana (He)

Case	With case ending	English
Nominative	aayana	Him
Accusative	aayana nu or aayana	Him
Dative	aayana kosam / aayana ki	For him
Genitive	aayana yokka or aayana	His
Genitive	aayanadhi (possessive pronoun)	His
Sociative	aayana tho or aayana dheggara	Along with him or near him
Ablative	aayana nunchi, aayana valana, aayana kante, aayana batti	From him, Because of him, than him, According to him.

Solutions

Exercise A

1) naa thammudu ki tea kavaali 2) naaku shop ki veLLaali ani undhi 3) I computer naa thandri kosam 4) a pusthakam naa anna kosam 5) naaku thinaali ani undhi 6) aameki vondaali ani undhi 7) naaku I pesarattu repu thinaali ani undhi 8) vaLLaku statue kavaali 9) naaku I roju mall ki veLLaali ani undhi 10) naaku ikkada thinaali ani undhi

Exercise B

1) I kukka niidhaa? 2) I pillu yevaradhi? 3) idhi mii/mii yokka bhojanam 4) idhi aayana / aayana yokka illu 5) idhi aame/aame yokka pusthakamaa? 6) adhi yevar car? 7) aavida aayana/aayana yokka bhaarya 8) aavida naa/naa yokka bhaarya 9) aayana naa/naa yokka bhartha 10) aayana mii/mii yokka bharthaa? 11) i kukka naadhi 12) a car miidhi 13) aayana naadhi 14) avi puvvulu aamedhi 15) i pencil aayanadhi.

Exercise C

1) nenu naa bhaarya tho breakfast thinnaanu 2) nenu naa bhartha tho shopping veLLaanu 3) nenu ninna naa friends tho unnaanu 4) pencil tho pusthakam undeedhi 5) nenu naa friend Maala tho kuurchuntaanu

Exercise D

1) nenu canada nunchi vochchaanu 2) nenu srilanka nunchi vochchaanu 3) nenu hotel nunchi vochchaanu 4) nenu inti nunchi vochchaanu 5) nenu shop nunchi vochchaanu

Exercise E

1) nenu aayana nunchi Jewels thiiskunnaanu 2) nenu vaLLa nunchi car thiiskunnaanu 3) nenu mii nunchi pusthakam thiiskunnaanu 4) nenu nii nunchi pencil thiiskunnaanu 5) nenu aame nunchi illu thiiskunnaanu

Exercise F

1) naaku naa friend nunchi letter vochchindhi 2) aavida Hyderabad nunchi vochchaaru 3) athanu podhdhun nunchi meeting lo unnadu 4) nenu London nunchi vochchaanu 5) nenu I pusthakam shop nunchi konnaanu.

Exercise G

1) e, 2) a, 3) c, 4) b, 5) f, 6) d.

Exercise H

1) a, 2) a, 3) c, 4) a, 5) b, 6) c, 7) b, 8) b, 9) b, 10) a, 11) c, 12) a, 13) b, 14) b, 15) a.

Exercise I

1) athanu chair lo kuurchunnaadu

2) Fridge lo koncham paalu unnaayi

3) aame balla kindha dhakundhi

4) pilli counter nunchi dhukindhi

5) athanu bridge miidha nadipaadu

6) aame aame ring beach lo pogotukundhi

7) i pusthakam antony dhi

8) vaaLLu chettu pakkana kuurchunnaadu

9) meemu I roju gym lo parigeduthunnaamu

10) suryudu mabbulu meedha unnaadu

11) aame office dhaggara untundhi

12) athanu cheruvu lo iidhaadu

13) nenu viidhi lo thirigaanu

14) Car tunnel dwara veLLindhi

15) naaku maa friend nunchi package vochchindhi

16) aame puulu kitiki pakkana pettindhi

17) bhojanam balla miida petti undhi

18) nenu conference ki samayaniki vosthaanu

19) pedhdha varsham tharuvatha baseball aata radhdhu chesaaru

20) John athani homework mancham kindha marchipoyaadu

21) athanu koncham sahayam tho gelichaadu

22) nenu athanini podhdhunna aidhu gantalaku park lo kalisaanu

LESSON 10: NEGATION

In Telugu, we use different forms of negation, which will be discussed one by one here.

1) vodhdhu / odhdhu (do not want, do not need), In some places people use the word 'vodhdhu' and in some places people use the word 'odhdhu'; it all depends on the accent: This word is the complete opposite of kavaali (want), **'vodhdhu'** means you don't want to do something or you don't need something.

Examples:

a) miiku coffee kavaalaa?

lit: for you coffee want.

t: Do you want coffee?

b) naaku coffee kavaali

lit: for me coffee want.

t: I want coffee

c) naaku coffee vodhdhu

lit: for me coffee do not want.

t: I don't want coffee

d) miiku coffee kavaalaa vodhdhaa?

lit: for me coffee do want do not want.

t: Do you want coffee or not?

e) vaallaku bhojanam vodhdhu

lit: for them breakfast do not want.

t: they don't want breakfast

f) athaniki paalu vodhdhu

lit: for him milk do not want.

t: he doesn't want milk

2) kaadhu (no), This word is the complete opposite of 'avunu' (yes), whenever you mean to say 'no' to someone you can use the Telugu word 'kaadhu'.

Example:

Dad: Jhonny, did you eat all the sugar?

Jhonny: kaadhu (nooo)

Examples:

a) idhi pen aa?

t: Is this a pen?

b) kaadhu, idhi pencil

t: No, this is a pencil.

c) miiku coffee kavaalaa?

lit: for you coffee want.

t: Do you want coffee?

d) kaadhu, naaku tea kavaali.

lit: no, for me tea want.

t: no, I want tea

e) miiku bhojanam kavaalaa?

lit: for you breakfast want.

t: Do you want breakfast?

f) kaadhu, naaku bhojanam vodhdhu.

lit: no, for me food don't want

t: no, I don't want food

Note: You can use 'avunu' in a different way as well, 'avunu' also provides the meaning 'It is true'.

Examples:

Man1: Yesterday, I saw an UFO.

Man2: avunaa? ('honestly?' or 'is it true?)

Man1: avunu ('yes, honestly' or 'Yes, it is true')

3) In Telugu we have a suffix for saying that, 'you are able to do it', 'you are unable to do it'.

- **-agala + -verb suffix** - able to
- **-ale + -verb suffix** - unable to / not able to

Note: This is a specific suffix, here you should use the verb suffix as per the subject. Kindly look into the examples below for more details for the same.

Examples:

a) nenu raayagalanu

Details: raayi (to write) + -agala (able to) + -nu (verb suffix of 'nenu') = raayagalanu

t: I am able to write

b) nenu raayalenu

Details: raayi (to write) + ale (unable to) + -nu (verb suffix of 'nenu') = raayalenu

t: I am unable to write / I am not able to write

c) meemu raayagalamu

Details: raayi (to write) + -agala (able to) + -mu (verb suffix of 'meemu') = raayagalamu

t: we are able to write

d) meemu raayalemu

Details: raayi (to write) + ale (unable to) + -mu (verb suffix of 'meemu') = raayalemu

t: we are unable to write / we are not able to write

e) nuvvu raayagalavaa?

Details: raayi (to write) + -agala (able to) + -vu (verb suffix of 'nuvvu') = raayagalavu

t: are you able to write?

f) nuvvu raayalevu

Details: raayi (to write) + ale (unable to) + -vu (verb suffix of 'nuvvu') = raayalevu

t: You are unable to write / You are not able to write

g) athanu raayagaladu

Details: raayi (to write) + -agala (able to) + -du (verb suffix of 'athanu') = raayagaladu

t: He is able to write

h) athanu raayaledu

Details: raayi (to write) + ale (unable to) + -du (verb suffix of 'athanu') = raayaledu

t: He is unable to write / He is not able to write

4a) In Telugu, in order to make a question using "can" you just need to use the same without the additional 'a'. Please refer to the below examples for more clarity on this. This format of 'can' is frequently used in Telugu.

	Verb	Future tense	Request clause (you)
1	cheyyi	nenu chesthaanu	miiru chestharaa?
	To do	I will do	Can you do?
2	kuurcho	nenu kuurchuntaanu	miiru kuurchuntaraa?
	To sit	I will sit	Can you sit?
3	le	nenu lesthaanu	miiru lestharaa?
	To get up	I will get up	Can you get up?
4	vochcha	nenu vosthaanu	miiru vostharaa?
	To come	I will come	Can you come?
5	veLLu	nenu veLthaanu	miiru veLtharaa?
	To go	I will go	Can you go?
6	aaduko	nenu aadukuntaanu	miiru aadukuntaraa?
	To play	I will play	Can you play?
7	raayi	nenu raasthaanu	miiru raastharaa?
	To write	I will write	Can you write?
8	parigeththu	nenu parigeduthaanu	miiru parigedutharaa?
	To run	I will run	Can you run?
9	kadugu	nenu kaduguthaanu	miiru kadugutharaa?
	To wash	I will wash	Can you wash?

As you saw in the above examples, I simply removed the letter 'a' from all the conjugated verbs in the future tense in order to make a request, "can you".

Note: Whenever you change the subject of the sentence which contains the request you need to change the last suffix accordingly.

For example:

	Request clause (he)	Request clause (we)	Request clause (you)
1	athanu chesthadaa?	meemu chesthamaa?	nuvvu chesthavaa?
	Can he do?	Can we do?	Can you do?
2	athanu kuurchuntadaa?	meemu kuurchuntamaa?	nuvvu kuurchuntavaa?
	Can he sit?	Can we sit?	Can you sit?
3	athanu lesthadaa?	meemu lesthamaa?	nuvvu lesthavaa?
	Can he get up?	Can we get up?	Can you get up?
4	athanu vosthadaa?	meemu vosthamaa?	nuvvu vosthavaa?
	Can he come?	Can we come?	Can you come?
5	athanu veLthadaa?	meemu veLthamaa?	nuvvu veLthavaa?
	Can he go?	Can we go?	Can you go?
6	athanu aadukuntadaa?	meemu aadukuntamaa?	nuvvu aadukuntavaa?
	Can he play?	Can we play?	Can you play?
7	athanu raasthadaa?	meemu raasthamaa?	nuvvu raasthavaa?
	Can he write?	Can we write?	Can you write?
8	athanu parigeduthadaa?	meemu parigeduthamaa?	nuvvu parigeduthavaa?
	Can he run?	Can we run?	Can you run?
9	athanu kaduguthadaa?	meemu kaduguthamaa?	nuvvu kaduguthavaa?
	Can he wash?	Can we wash?	Can you wash?

In Detail:

meemu chesthaamu - we will do

meemu chesthamu - we can do

meemu chesthamaa? - can we do?

147

4b) There is also another way of representing 'can' in Telugu. This form is used pretty rarely. This form is very precise; it is used when somebody wants to know for sure.

- -adam + kudhuruthundhi - Can do
- -adam + kudharadhu - Cannot
- -adam + kudharaledhu - Could not

Wherever you make a statement or question using the above forms, you should always use the Dative case for the subject. e.g., naaku, miiku etc.

Examples:

a) athaniki parigeththadam kudharaledhu.

lit: for him run could not.

t: he could not run.

In Detail:

athaniki - for him (Dative case)

parigeththu (to run) (verb) + -adam= parigeththadam

kudharadhu - Could not

b) athaniki parigeththadam kudharadhu.

lit: for him run cannot.

t: he cannot run.

c) athaniki parigeththadam kudhuruthundhi.

lit: for him run can.

t: he can run.

d) athaniki vondadam kudharaledhu.

lit: for him cook could not.

t: he could not cook.

e) naaku paadadam kudharadhu.

lit: for me sing cannot.

t: I cannot sing.

f) naaku matlaadadam kudhuruthundhi.

lit: for me speak can.

t: I can speak.

g) athaniki paadadam kudhuruthundhaa?

lit: for he sing can.

t: can he sing?

h) avunu, athaniki paadadam kudhuruthundhi.

lit: Yes, for he sing can.

t: Yes, he can sing.

More Examples:

Case	Verb	Capability	Telugu	English
athaniki	paadadam	kudhuruthundhi	athaniki paadadam kudhuruthundhi	He can sing
athaniki	paadadam	kudharadhu	athaniki paadadam kudharadhu	He cannot sing
athaniki	paadadam	kudharaledhu	athaniki paadadam kudharaledhu	He could not sing
naaku	aadadam	kudhuruthundhi	naaku aadadam kudhuruthundhi	I can play
naaku	aadadam	kudharadhu	naaku aadadam kudharadhu	I cannot play
naaku	aadadam	kudharaledhu	naaku aadadam kudharaledhu	I could not play

5) We have a separate word for saying that, 'Like', 'don't like'.

- **ishtam** - Like
- **ishtam undadhu** - Do not like
- **ishtam ledhu** - Did not like

The difference between 'ishtam undadhu' and 'ishtam ledhu' is, when you say 'ishtam undadhu' - 'It means you will never like it and you haven't tried it as well'. When you say 'ishtam ledhu', 'It means you have tried it but you didn't like it'. You should use the Dative case for the subject like before.

Examples:

a) naaku chocolate ishtam.

lit: for me chocolate like.

t: I like chocolate.

b) naaku chocolate ishtam undadhu.

lit: for me chocolate don't like.

t: I don't like chocolate.

c) naaku athanu ishtam undadhu.

lit: for me him don't like

t: I don't like him.

d) naaku a shop ishtam undadhu.

lit: for me that shop don't like

t: I don't like that shop.

e) naaku i dress ishtam ledhu.

lit: for me this dress didn't like

t: I didn't like this dress.

f) naaku nii vanta ishtam ledhu.

lit: for me your cooking didn't like

t: I don't like your cooking

g) aameki chicken ishtam undadhu.

lit: for her chicken does not like

t: She doesn't like chicken.

6) We have a separate word for saying that, 'know', 'don't know'.

- **thelusu** - Know
- **theliyadhu** - Do not know

You should use the Dative case for the subject while you use the above words.

Examples:

a) naaku Cricket thelusu.

lit: for me cricket know

t: I know Cricket.

b) naaku vondu thelusu.

lit: for me to cook know

t: I know to cook.

c) naaku vaallanu thelusu

lit: for me them know.

t: I know them

d) naaku aayananu theliyadhu.

lit: for me him don't know

t: I don't know him.

e) naaku a sthalamu theliyadhu.

lit: for me that place don't know

t: I don't know that place.

f) naaku vondadam theliyadhu.

lit: for me to cook don't know

t: I don't know to cook.

g) naaku a address theliyadhu.

lit: for me that address don't know

t: I don't know that address.

h) niiku / miiku athanu thelusaa?

lit: for you him know

t: Do you know him?

7) We have a separate word for saying that, 'understood', 'don't understand'.

- **ardham ayindhi** - Understood
- **ardham kaadhu** - Do not understand
- **ardham kaaledhu** - Did not understand

You should use the Dative case for the subject while you use the above words.

Examples:

a) naaku ardham ayindhi

lit: for me understood

t: I understood

b) naaku Spanish ardham kaadhu

lit: for me Spanish don't understand

t: I don't understand Spanish.

c) naaku Telugu ardham ayindhi

lit: for me Telugu understood

t: I understood Telugu.

d) naaku Adjectives ardham kaaledhu

lit: for me adjectives did not understood

t: I didn't understand adjectives.

e) naaku Physics ardham ayindhi

lit: for me Physics understood

t: I understood Physics

f) naaku Chemistry ardham kaadhu

lit: for me Chemistry don't understand

t: I don't understand Chemistry.

g) naaku mathematics ardham ayindhi

lit: for me mathematics understood

t: I understood mathematics.

h) naaku rocket science ardham kaaledhu

lit: for me rocket science did not understood

t: I didn't understand rocket science.

8) We have a separate word for saying, 'there is', 'there is not'.

- **undhi** - Is there
- **ledhu** - There is not

ledhu (don't have, is not there, not available, does not exist), This word is the complete opposite to 'undhi' (have, is there, available, exist), It means you don't have something or something is not available or simply it doesn't exist.

undadhu (will not have, will not be there, will not be available, will not exist).

Examples:

a) mii dhaggara pen undhaa?

lit: with you pen have.

t: Do you have pen with you?

b) naa dhaggara / naa tho pen ledhu

lit: with me pen don't have.

t: I don't have a pen with me.

c) Hospital aadhivaaram untundhaa?

lit: Hospitals on Sunday will be there

t: will there be hospitals on Sunday? / Will the hospitals be open on Sunday?

d) Hospital aadhivaaram undadhu.

lit: Hospitals on Sunday will not be there

t: Hospitals will not be there on Sunday? / Hospitals will be open on Sunday?

e) repu shop undhaa?

lit: Tomorrow shop is there?

t: Is there shop tomorrow?

f) repu shop undhi?

lit: Tomorrow shop there is

t: There is shop tomorrow

g) naa dhaggara / naa tho chocolate ledhu

lit: with me chocolate don't have.

t: I don't have a chocolate with me.

9) We have a separate word for saying, 'enough', 'not enough'.

- **chaalu** - Enough
- **saripothundhi** - sufficient
- **saripodhu** - Not enough, not sufficient

Examples:

a) naaku chaalu

lit: for me enough

t: Enough for me

b) naaku saripodhu

lit: for me not enough

t: Not enough for me

c) naaku i Ice cream sarupodhu

lit: for me this Ice cream is not enough

t: This Ice cream is not enough for me

d) naaku i bhojanam saripothundhi

lit: for me this food is sufficient

t: This food is sufficient for me

e) naaku i bhojanam chaalu

lit: for me this food is enough

t: This food is enough for me

f) vaLLaku intha dabbu chaalu

lit: for them this much money is enough

t: This much money is enough for them

g) vaLLaku intha dabbu saripodhu

lit: for them this much money is not enough

t: This much money is not enough for them

10a) Verb Negation:

The Verb negation is made by adding either of the suffixes -odhdhu (informal) or -odhdhandi (formal) to the root of the verb. It's used to command or request someone or something not to do it.

Examples:

Verb	Informal verb negation	English	Formal verb negation	English
thinu	thinnodhdhu	don't eat	thinnodhdhandi	Please don't eat
piluvu	piluvodhdhu	don't call	piluvodhdhandi	Please don't call
chuudu	chuudodhdhu	don't see	chuudodhdhandi	Please don't see
kuurchu	kuurchodhdhu	don't sit	kuurchodhdhandi	Please don't sit
ivvu	ivvodhdhu	don't give	ivvodhdhandi	Please don't give
chadhuvu	chadhuvodhdhu	don't see	chadhuvodhdhandi	Please don't see
raayi	raayodhdhu	don't write	raayodhdhandi	Please don't write
cheyyi	cheyyodhdhu	don't do	cheyyodhdhandi	Please don't do

a) naa pusthakam ivvodhdhandi

lit: my book please don't give

t: Please don't give my book.

b) akkada veLLodhdhu

Detail: veLLu (to go) + odhdhu = veLLodhdhu

lit: there don't go

t: don't go there

10b) Verb Negation:

When you want to command someone that he/she should not perform that activity, then you should use the suffix '-akuudadhu'

-akuudadhu - Should not, shall not

Examples:

a) miiru naa pusthakam ivvakuudadhu

lit: you my book shouldn't give

t: you shouldn't give my book.

b) aayana veLLakuudadhu

Detail: veLLu (to go) + akuudadhu= veLLakuudadhu

t: he shouldn't go

Examples:

Pronoun	Verb	Suffix	Command	English
nenu (I)	thinu	-akuudadhu	thinnakuudadhu	I shouldn't eat
nuvvu (you)	piluvu	-akuudadhu	piluvakuudadhu	You shouldn't call
miiru (You)	chuudu	-akuudadhu	chuudakuudadhu	You shouldn't see
athanu (he)	kuurchu	-akuudadhu	kuurchakuudadhu	He shouldn't sit
aayana (he)	ivvu	-akuudadhu	ivvakuudadhu	He shouldn't give
aame (she)	chadhuvu	-akuudadhu	chadhuvakuudadhu	She shouldn't see
aavida (she)	raayi	-akuudadhu	raayakuudadhu	She shouldn't write
vaaLLu (they)	cheyyi	-akuudadhu	cheyyakuudadhu	They shouldn't do

11) Past/Present Tense Verb Negation:

The verb can be negated in both Past and Present tense using the suffix -ledhu being added to the infinitive of the verb.

Examples:

Pronoun	Verb (Infinitive)	Tense negation suffix	Negated verb in Past and Present Tense	English
nenu	cheyyi (cheyye)	-ledhu	cheyyeledhu	I didn't do
miiru	raa (raa)	-ledhu	raaledhu	You didn't come
athanu	raayi (raaye)	-ledhu	raayeledhu	He didn't write
aayana	veLLu (velle)	-ledhu	veLLeledhu	He didn't go
aame	muyyi (muyye)	-ledhu	muyyeledhu	She didn't close
vaaLLu	piluvu (piluve)	-ledhu	piluveledhu	They didn't call
manamu	cheppu (cheppe)	-ledhu	cheppeledhu	We didn't tell

a) miiru naa pusthakam thiiskeledhu

lit: you my book didn't take

t: You didn't take my book

b) nenu meeting ki raaledhu

lit: I for the meeting didn't come

t: I didn't come for the meeting

Note: During negation, you would use the verb 'raa' instead of 'vochcha' for the English verb 'to come'.

c) nenu naa homework raayeledhu

lit: I my homework didn't writ

t: I didn't write my homework

12) Future Tense Verb Negation:

The verb can be negated in Future tense using the suffix '-a' being added along with the verb suffix of the respective pronoun. e verb.

Note: Unlike Past/Present tense verb negation, for future tense negation, the ending will change based on the subject/person.

Examples:

Pronoun	Verb	Future tense negation suffix	Verb suffix (PNG)	Negated verb in future tense	English
nenu	cheyyi	-a-	-nu	cheyyanu	I will not do
miiru	thinu	-a-	-ru	thinnaru	You will not eat
athanu	raayi	-a-	-du	raayadu	He will not write
aayana	veLLu	-a-	-ru	veLLaru	He will not go
aame	muyyi	-a-	-dhu	muyyadhu	She will not close
vaaLLu	piluvu	-a-	-ru	piluvaru	They will not call
manamu	cheppu	-a-	-mu	cheppamu	We will not tell
avi/ivi	thinu	-a-	-vu	thinnavu	It will not eat

a) nenu aayana tho veLLanu

lit: I along with him will not go

t: I will not go along with him

b) aame vaaLLa tho thinadhu

lit: she along with them will not eat

t: She will not eat along with them.

13) Conditional Negation:

Conditional negation is used as an equivalent of using 'If' in English. If clause in a sentence is created by adding the suffix -kapothe to verb root.

Example:

a) Homework cheyyakapoththe nuvvu school ki raavodhdhu

Details: cheyyi (to do) + kapothe = cheyyakapothe

lit: Homework if you don't do you to the school don't come.

t: If you don't write home work, don't come to school.

b) nenu veLLakapoththe aame yedusthundhi.

Details: veLLu (to go) + kapothe = veLLakapothe

t: If I don't go, she will cry

Note: There are many other forms of 'If' clause in Telugu, but the above suffix is the most common one. Since they are rarely used, I didn't provide any details about them.

Exercises:

A) Match the following Telugu word in the first column with the appropriate English translation form in the second column.

1	Don't know	a	ledhu
2	Know	b	Ishtam
3	Like	c	ishtam ledhu
4	Don't like	d	ardham ayindhi
5	Understand	e	ardham kaaledhu
6	Could not do	f	cheyya kodadhu
7	Commanding not to do	g	kavaali
8	There is no or does not exist	h	vodhdhu
9	Want	i	theliyadhu
10	Don't want	j	thelusu
11	Don't understand	k	cheyyadhdhu

B) Fill in the blanks with the right word or suffix.

Example: naaku i letter _____ (I understand this letter)

Answer: ardham ayindhi

1. niiku i prashna ku samadhaanam _____ (Do you know the answer for this question?)

2. idhu athaniki _____ (Please don't give him)

3. a kukka _____ (That dog won't bite)

4. naaku repu pani _____ (I have work tomorrow)

5. naaku i aata _____ (I don't like this game)

6. naaku repu pani _____ (I don't have work tomorrow)

7. naaku i prashna ki samadhaanam _____ (I don't know the answer for this question)

8. athanu niillu _____ (He will not drink water)

160

9. ayana niillu _____ (He will not drink water)

10. i shop lo coffee _____ (Don't drink coffee in this shop)

11. naaku i letter _____ (I don't understand this letter)

C) Translate the following.

1. Please don't eat food in this shop

2. Do you know that house on that street?

3. He will not drink at work

4. That dog won't run

5. could not speak with him

6. I understand this game

7. I have a bag

8. I don't like this food

9. I like that girl

10. I don't know him

11. Please don't take this phone

12. I am able to speak to the boy

13. I don't understand this game

14. I don't have a bag

15. This coffee is enough for me

16. I don't like him.

17. That tea is not enough for me.

Solutions

Exercise A

1) i, 2) j, 3) b, 4) c, 5) d, 6) k, 7) f, 8) a, 9) g, 10) h, 11) e.

Exercise B

1) thelusaa 2) ivvodhdhandi 3) karavadhu 4) undhi 5) ishtam ledhu 6) ledhu 7) theliyadhu 8) thaagadu 9) thaagaru 10) thaagodhdhu 11) ardham kaadhu

Exercise C

1) i shop lo bhojanam cheyyoddhu 2)a viidhi lo a illu miiku thelusaa? 3) athanu office lo thaagadu 4) a kukka parigeththadhu 5) nenu athani tho matladalenu 6) naaku i aata ardham ayindhi 7) naa dhaggara bag undhi 8)naaku i bhojanam ishtam ledhu 9) naaku a ammayi nachchindhi 10) naaku athanu theliyadhu 11) I phone thiiskodhdhu 12) nenu athani tho matladagalanu 13) naaku i aata ardham kaadhu 14) naa dhaggara bag ledhu 15) naaku i coffee chaalu 16) maaku athanu ishtam ledhu 17) a tea naaku saripodhu

LESSON 11: IMPORTANT SUFFIXES

1) Conjunction ('And' and 'Also')

When you add the suffix **-kuuda** to a noun or an adverb, it will give you the meaning of 'also' in English. If you add it to a succession of two or more words then it will coordinate and join them together in a sentence, equivalent to English 'and'.

Note: In English, when a group of nouns is conjoined together, we add 'and' at the end, e.g., 'Mary, Peter, Kathy, and Ronald went to church'. As you see in the example I added 'and' at the end of the conjunction, whereas in Telugu you have to add the suffix -kuuda to each and every noun, but this is optional. You can also make a statement without using the suffix '-kuuda' and it gives the same meaning.

Example:

a) naaku tii kuuda ivvandi

lit: to me tea also please give

t: Please give me tea also

Vocabulary: pesarattu, dhosa, sambhaar are a type of food in Andhra Pradesh

b) naaku tii, coffii, dhosa, pesarattu, sambhaar ivvandi.

lit: to me tea and coffee and dosa and pesarattu and sambar please give

t: Please give me tea, coffee, dosa, pesarattu and sambar.

Note: Using the suffix -kuuda for referring 'And' is optional, you can even make a sentence without using the suffix -kuuda and it still means the same.

c) naaku okka koduku kuthutru unnaaru

lit: for me one son and a daughter are there

t: I have a son and a daughter.

d) nenu I roju veLLi repu vosthaanu

lit: I today go tomorrow will come

t: I will go today and come tomorrow.

2) Disjunction ('or')

There are different ways of adding 'or' in a Telugu sentence, so please don't stress too much about it. You can use any one of the methods I have given below and the other person will be able to understand you well. Everything I have mentioned below are frequently used, it all depends on the person and their dialect.

a) When there is more than one interrogative noun, then you will add the word **'kavaalaa'** **(want)** to both of them to mention 'or' in between them.

Example:

miiku tii kavaalaa coffii kavaalaa

lit: for you tea want or coffee want

t: Do you want tea or coffee?

b) Alternatively, you can also use the word **'ledha'** (or else, otherwise).

Example:

1) miiku tii ledha coffii kavaalaa

lit: for you tea or coffee want

t: Do you want tea or coffee?

2) miiku a room ledha I room kavaalaa

lit: for you that room or this room want

t: Do you want that room or this room?

Another Example:

miiru vostharaa raaraa?

lit/t: Will you come or not

3) More Coordination Words:

a) kaani (But):

Examples:

1) naaku athanu ishtam kaani nenu athani tho matlaadanu

lit: for me he like but I with him don't speak

t: I like him but I don't speak to him

2) aayana vanta chesthaaru kaani adhi bhagha ledhu.

lit: He is doing cooking but that good not

t: He is cooking but it is not good

Note: Unlike English, in Telugu you can literally say "doing cooking" instead of just saying "cooking". "cooking" and "doing cooking" both statements makes sense in Telugu but "doing cooking" is the most commonly used expression in Telugu.

b) andhukani (So, because of that):

Examples:

1) nenu ninna bhojanam thinnaledhu andhukani naaku ippudu akali ga undhi

lit: I yesterday breakfast didn't eat so for me now feeling hungry

t: Yesterday I didn't eat breakfast so I am feeling hungry now.

Vocabulary: akali - hungry, ga - being, akalai ga - being hungy.

Note: In Telugu, one doesn't just say hungry, you should only say 'being hungry'.

2) naaku ninna class undhi andhukani nenu party ki veLLaledhu

lit: for me yesterday class was there because of that I didn't go to the party

t: I had a class yesterday because of that I didn't go to the party.

c) endhukante (because):

Examples:

1) naaku ippudu chaala akali ga undhi endhukante nenu ninna thinnaledhu

lit: for me now very feeling hungry because I yesterday didn't eat.

t: I am feeling very hungry now because I didn't eat yesterday.

2) aame naa tho matlaadadhu endhukante nenu ninna aame tho godava paddaanu

t: She will not speak to me because I fought with her yesterday.

d) tharuvatha (after that):

Note: If there is a verb before the word 'tharuvatha', then you should add the suffix '-ina' to that verb.

Examples:

1) nenu shopki veLLina tharuvatha coffii konnaanu

lit: I to the shop went after that I bought coffee.

t: I went to the shop after that I bought coffee

2) nenu pusthakam chadhivina tharuvatha movie chusaanu.

lit: I book read after that I the film saw

t: I read the book after that I saw the film

4) Asking and Giving Permission:

There are different ways of asking for permission in Telugu, the below mentioned examples are some of the frequently used forms in Telugu.

Examples:

a) manamu shopki veLdhaamaa?

lit: we to the shop shall we go

t: Shall we go to the shop?

b) nenu pusthakam konnochaa?

lit: I book shall I buy

t: Shall I buy the book?

c) nenu mii intiki raavachaa

lit: I your house shall I come

t: Shall I come to your house?

d) nenu matlaadochaa?

t/lit: Shall I speak?

e) miiru matlaadochu

t/lit: You shall speak?

5) Plural

The plural form is a bit complicated in Telugu than in English. The plural form in English is very simple, we just have to add the suffix '-s' to the noun (there are few exceptions though).

But in Telugu, the suffix depends on the ending of the noun. If you ask me why do we do this, the answer is quite simple: to make the pronunciation easier and more synchronized. This will be a little difficult initially but please bear with me, as your keep practicing Telugu, depending on the ending of the noun you would automatically use the right plural suffix.

If not, you would still be able to recognize that you are making a mistake by observing whether it is difficult for you to pronounce the noun with the plural suffix. If it's easier for you to pronounce, then you are using the right plural suffix. If not, then you are using the wrong suffix. Even native Telugu speakers would use the same method initially, but we don't realize it anymore because it became so natural for us.

The above method is similar to articles in English, e.g., If I say 'There is a Elephant' in English, immediately you would realize that I have made a mistake, I should have said 'an Elephant' not 'a Elephant'. I don't know about you but English is a second language to me, so I learned it as a rule that whenever a noun starts with a vowel, we should use the article 'an', If not then 'a' (there are few exceptions though). Initially I used to check the first letter of the noun but at one point it became so natural that I don't even have to check, it became like an intuition to me whether I should use 'a' or 'an'.

The same concept applies to you as well; initially you may have to think about which suffix to use in Telugu. But the more you practice Telugu, the more these rules become natural to you.

The rules below are for using the right suffix to make a noun plural in Telugu. There are 6 suffixes in total to make a noun plural in Telugu, of course, with few exceptions as usual.

The below are the list of rules to make a Telugu word plural.

1) For more than 50% of the nouns in Telugu, you just have to add the suffix -lu' to make them plural. So, when you are not sure which suffix to use to make a noun plural in Telugu, then just add the suffix '-lu' to it. There is a higher possibility that you got it right.

Examples:

Singular form	English	Plural form	English
balla	Bench	ballalu	Benches
siisaa	Bottle	siisaalu	Bottles
puvvu	Flower	puvvulu	Flowers
meeka	Goat	meekalu	Goats
navvu	Laugh	navvulu	Laughs
kitiki	Window	kitikiilu	Windows
bhaarya	Wife	bhaaryalu	Wives
aaku	Leaf	aakulu	Leaves
stree	Lady	streelu	Ladies
yeluka	Rat	yelukalu	Rats
bomma	Toy	bommalu	Toys
gorre	Sheep	gorrelu	Sheep
jinka	Deer	jinkalu	Deer
padava	Boat	padavalu	Boats
cheepa	Fish	cheepalu	Fishes
thalupu	Door	thalupulu	Doors
goda	Wall	godalu	Walls

2) In order to make Telugu words ending with 'am' plural, you have to replace the letters 'am' with the suffix 'aalu'. **Example:** vanam (Garden) and its plural form will be 'vanaalu' (Gardens).

Singular form	English	Plural form	English
pusthakam	Book	pusthakaalu	Books
desham	Country	dhesaalu	Countries
pathakam	Medal	pathakaalu	medals
sahaayam	Help	sahaayaalu	Helps
gadiyaaram	Watch	gadiyaaraalu	Watches
jiivitham	Life	jiivithaalu	Lives
nagaram	Cities	nagaraalu	Cities
paadham	Foot	paadhaalu	Feet
prayaanam	Journey	prayaanaalu	Journies
vimaanam	Flight	vimaanaalu	Flights

3) In order to make Telugu words ending with 'i' plural, you have to replace the letters 'i' with the suffix 'ulu'.

Singular form	English	Plural form	English
kaaki	Crow	kaakulu	Crows
pakshi	Bird	pakshulu	Birds
puli	Tiger	pululu	Tigers
kothi	Monkey	kothulu	Monkies
pilli	Cat	pillulu	Cats
nadi	River	nadulu	Rivers

| vyakthi | Person | vyakthulu | Persons |
| kaththi | Knife | kaththulu | Knives |

4) In order to make Telugu words ending with 'di' and 'du' plural, you have to replace the letters 'di' and 'du' with the suffix 'LLu'.

Singular form	English	Plural form	English
gudi	Temple	guLLu	Temples
badi	School	baLLu	Schools
mudi	Knot	muLLu	Knots
pachchadi	Pickle	pachchaLLu	Pickles
guudu	Nest	guuLLu	Nests
yeedu	Year	yeeLLu	Years

5) In order to make Telugu words ending with 'yyi' plural, you have to replace the letters 'yyi' with the suffix 'thulu'.

Singular form	English	Plural form	English
cheyyi	Hand	chethulu	Hands
nuyyi	Well	nuuthulu	Wells
goyyi	Pit	gothulu	Pits

6) In order to make Telugu words ending with 'li', 'nnu' and 'lu' plural, you have to replace the letters 'li', 'nnu' and 'lu' with the suffix 'LLu'.

Singular form	English	Plural form	English
kaalu	Leg	kaaLLu	Legs
mosali	Crocodile	mosaLLu	Crocodiles

veelu	Finger	veeLLu	Finger
vakili	Door way	vaakiLLu	Doorways
naagali	Plough	naagaLLu	Ploughs
kannu	Eye	kaLLu	Eyes
pannu	Tooth	paLLu	Teeth

Note: The above rules I have mentioned are not concrete. There will always be some exceptional cases where they will not follow a pattern and you have to learn them as it is.

Example:

Singular form	English	Plural form	English
baaludu	Boy	baaluru	Boys
vaadu	He	vaaru	He
purushudu	Man	purushulu	Men
devudu	God	devuLLu	Gods
poyyi	Stove	poyyilu	Stoves

6) andharu/anni (all):

This word/suffix usually comes after the noun; this can be used as a suffix and as a word.

The word 'andharam' is used specifically while referring to a person and the word 'anni' is used while referring to objects and animals

Examples:

manamu (we) + andharam (all) =manamu andharam (We all).

meemu (we) + andharam (all) =meemu andharam (We all).

vaaLLu (they) + andharam (all) = vaLLu andharam (They all).

ivi (these) + anni (all) = ivi anni (These all).

avi (those) + anni (all) = avi anni (Those all).

7) inka (still, yet), inka ledhu (not yet).

Examples:

a) Scenario: Let's take a scenario of a father and son in train:

Son: Have we reached yet?

Father: inka koncham samayam (Still a little more time).

Son: Have we reached yet?

Father: inka ledhu (Not yet)

b) Father: ayindhaa?

lit/t: Have you finished? / is it over.

c) Son: inka ledhu

lit/t: Not yet.

d) Father: inka fridge lo Ice cream undhaa?

lit/t: Is there still ice cream in the fridge?

e) Son: ledhu

lit/t: Nope.

Exercises:

A) Match the following nouns and pronouns in the first column with the appropriate plural form in the second column.

1	cheppu	a	gaajulu
2	pelli	b	varshaalu
3	mancham	c	metlu
4	cup	d	ammayilu
5	ammayi	e	abbaayilu
6	abbaayi	f	cupplu
7	mettu	g	manchaalu
8	varsham	h	pelliLLu
9	gaaju	i	cheppulu

B) Translate the following sentences from English to Telugu using appropriate plural form.

1) I kept my slippers in the slipper stand

2) I bite with my teeth.

3) I see with my eyes

4) I pray with my hands

5) I have two houses

6) There are five crocodiles

7) Two teams played form Rajasthan

C) Match the following Telugu word and suffix in the first column with the appropriate English translation form in the second column.

1	tharuvatha	a	But
2	endhukante	b	Because of that
3	kuuda	c	So
4	anni	d	At least
5	aina	e	Not yet
6	andhukani	f	Still
7	inka	g	All
8	kaani	h	Also
9	inka ledhu	i	After that

D) Fill in the blanks with the right word or suffix.

Example: _____ naaku akali ga undhi (Because I am feeling hungry)

Answer: endhukante

1. nenu repu vosthaanu _____ athani tho matlaadanu (I will come tomorrow but I will not speak to him)

2. ninna nenu parigeththaledhu _____ nenu I roju parigeduthunnaanu (Yesterday I didn't run because of that I am running now)

3. vaaLLu ippudu thintunnaaru _____ vaaLLaku akali ga undhi (They are eating now because they are hungry)

4. _____ beachki _____? (Shall we all go to the beach?)

5. vaaLLu aadaaru _____ paadaaru (They danced after that they sang)

6. naaku _____ bhojanam kavaali (I also want food)

7.athanu bhagha thitaadu _____ athaniki vanta raadhu (He eats well but he doesn't know to cook)

8. naaku _____ _____ kavaali (I want book and pen)

9. naaku a pusthakam nachchaledhu _____ nenu a pusthakam konaledhu (I didn't like that book because of that I didn't buy it)

10. nenu nii tho _____? (Shall I speak with you?)

11. aame manchi niillu thaagi _____ aadukundhi (She drank water after that she played)

E) Translate the following.

1. Yesterday I didn't walk because of that I am walking now

2. They laughed after that they sang

3. I will come but I will not drink with him

4. I also want to study

5. She drank water after that she laughed

6. I didn't like that coffee because of that I didn't buy it

7. Shall we all go to the mall?

8. They are drinking now because they are thirsty

9. He talks well but he doesn't know to sing.

10. I want cat and dog

11. Shall I speak to you?

Solutions

Exercise A

1	cheppu (Slipper)	=	cheppulu (Slippers)
2	pelli (Marriage)	=	pelliLLu (Marriages)
3	mancham (Cot)	=	manchaalu (Cots)
4	cup (Cup)	=	cupplu (Cups)
5	ammayi (Girl)	=	ammayilu (Girls)
6	abbaayi (Boy)	=	abbaayilu (Boys)
7	mettu (Step)	=	metlu (Steps)
8	varsham (Rain)	=	varshaalu (Rain)
9	gaaju (Bangle)	=	gaajulu (Bangles)

Exercise B

1) nenu naa cheppulu cheppula stand lo pettanu 2) nenu naa paLLatho korikaanu 3) nenu naa kalla tho chusthaanu 4) nenu naa chethulu tho prardhana chesthaanu 5) naaku rendu illu unnaayi 6) akkada aidhu mosallu unnaayi 7) Rajasthan nunchi rendu jattlu aadaayi

Exercise C

1) i, 2) c, 3) h, 4) g, 5) d, 6) b, 7) f, 8) a, 9) e.

Exercise D

1) kaani 2) andhukani 3) endhukante 4) manam andharam, veLLochchaa 5) tharuvatha 6) kuuda 7) kaani 8) pusthakam, pennu 9) andhukani 10) matlaadochchaa? 11) tharuvatha

Exercise E

1) ninna nenu nadavaledhu andhukani nenu ippudu nadusthunaanu 2) vaaLLu navvaaru tharuvatha paadaaru 3) nenu vosthaanu kaani athani tho thaaganu 4) naaku kuuda chadhavaali ani undhi 5) aame manchi niillu thagina tharuvatha navvindhi 6) naaku a coffee ishtam ledhu andhukani nenu konaledhu 7) manam andharam mall ki veLdhaamaa 8) vaaLLu ippudu manchi niillu thaaguthunnaaru endhukante vaaLLaku dhaaham ga undhi 9) athanu bhagha matlaaduthaadu kani paadadam theliyadhu 10) naaku pilli kukka kavaali 11) nenu nii tho matlaadochchaa.

LESSON 12: ADJECTIVES AND ADVERBS

An adjective is a word that describes or modifies a noun in a sentence. An Adjective is used with noun to describe or to point out the person, animal, place or thing's color, shape, size, demonstrative, quality, number or quantity. To make it simple, an adjective is a word which is used along with a noun to add more to its meaning.

An adjective can be formed in Telugu by adding a suffix to a noun or a verb. The most commonly used suffixes to make a noun an adjective is '-aina' and '-ti'. Please note that there are some occasions where you don't have to add any suffix to a noun to make it as an Adjective and there are some occasions where you can either use the suffix '-aina' or '-ti' to create an adjective. There are also some occasions where they don't follow the rules at all. I tried to form a pattern which is applicable for most of the adjectives and adverbs, but there are some exceptions.

Adjectives Made from Noun Using the Suffix '-aina':

1) Inherent or simple adjectives: There are only few Inherent adjectives in Telugu. These words have adjectival function but they are not derived from any other word. They are not derived from another word so it is best to memorize them as it, because there are only few of them but they are frequently used while making sentences.

Some Frequently used Inherent Adjectives are given below:

Inherent Adjective (Telugu)	English
manchi	Good
chedu	Bad
pedhdha	Big
chinna	Small
koncham	Little, some
koththa	New
paatha	Old

maamulga	Normally
chaala	Much/Very
konni	Some

2) Derived adjectives: These adjectives are created by taking a noun or a verb and adding an adverbial suffix to it, thus making it as an adjective. Most of the adjectives in Telugu belong to this category.

Category Wise Derived Adjectives are Given Below:

2a) Sizes:

Noun	Telugu	Adjective Suffix	Adjective	English
Circle	gundram	+ '-aina'	gundramaina	Circular
Depth	lothu	+ '-aina'	lothina	Deep
Length	podavu	+ '-aina'	podavaina	Long
Narrow	sannam	+ '-ti'	sannati	Narrow
Short	potti	+ '-aina'	pottaina	Short
Square	chadharam	+ '-aina'	chadharamaina	Square
Height	yeththu	+ '-aina'	yeththaina	Tall
Thick	mandham	+ '-aina'	mandhamaina	Thick
Skinny	sannam	+ '-ti'	sannati	Thin
Width	vedalpu	+ '-aina'	vedalpaina	Wide

2b) Taste:

Noun	Telugu	Adjective Suffix	Adjective	English
Taste	ruchi	+ '-aina'	ruchiaina	Tasty
Sweet	thiipi	+ '-aina'	thiipiaina	Sweet
Salt	uppu	+ '-ti'	uppati	Salty

Sour	pulla	+ '-aina', 'ti'	pullanaina	Sour
Spicy	ghaatu	+ '-aina'	ghaataina	Spicy
Hot	kaaram	+ '-aina'	kaaramaina	Hot
Bitter	cheedhu	+ '-aina'	cheedhaina	Bitter

2c) Qualities:

Noun	Telugu	Adjective Suffix	Adjective	English
Beauty	andham	+ '-aina'	andhamaina	Beautiful
Clean	subhram	+ '-aina'	subhramaina	Clean
Okay	sare	+ '-aina'	sariaina	Correct
Dark	chekati	no suffix	chekati	Dark
Difficult	kashtam	+ '-aina'	kashtamaina	Difficult
Dirt	muriki	no suffix	muriki	Dirty
Empty	khaali	no suffix	khaali	Empty
Expensive	khariidhu	+ '-aina'	khariidhaina	Expensive
Easy	thelika	no suffix	thelika	Easy
Speed	veegam	no suffix	veegamaina	Fast
Heavy	baruvu	+ '-aina'	baruvaina	Heavy
Less expensive	chavuka	no suffix	chavuka	Less expensive
Light	thelika	no suffix	thelika	Light
Silence	nishabdham	+ '-aina'	nishabdhamaina	Quiet
Slow	nidhaanam	no suffix	nidhaanam	Slow
Soft	methani	no suffix	methani	Soft

Ugly	vikrutham	+ '-aina'	vikruthamaina	Ugly
Weak	balaheenam	+ '-aina'	balaheenamaina	Weak
Wet	thadi	no suffix	thadi	Wet
Wrong	thappu	no suffix	thappu	Wrong
Young	yavvanam	+ '-aina'	yavvanamaina	Young

2d) Quantitative:

Noun	Telugu	Adjective Suffix	Adjective	English
Less	thakkuva	no suffix	thakkuva	Less
More	yekkuva	no suffix	yekkuva	More
Little	koncham	no suffix	koncham	Little
Some	konni	no suffix	konni	Some
Many, much	chaala	no suffix	chaala	Many or much

2e) Numeral:

Example: 'okka pusthakam' (a book), 'rendu bandhlu' (two vehicles).

Here the numbers which comes before the noun describes the quantity of the same. The numbers are adjective in this scenario.

2f) Color:

Noun	Telugu	Adjective Suffix	Adjective	English
Red	yeruppu	+ '-ani' or '-ti'	yerrati or yerrani	Red colour
Yellow	pasupupachcha	+ '-ani' or '-ti'	pasupupachchani or pasupupachchati	Yellow colour
Green	pachcha	+ '-ani' or '-ti'	pachchani or pachchati	Green colour
Blue	niilam	no suffix	niilam	Blue colour
Black	nallupu	+ '-ani' or '-ti'	nallati	Black colour

Example:

a) yerra godugu (Red umbrella)

b) niilam illu (Blue house)

Here the color which comes before the noun describes the quantity of the same. The colors are adjective in this scenario.

Note: As mentioned earlier, the adjective form of colors can also be represented in a different way when you use the suffix '-ina', '-ni' or '-ti' next to it.

Example:

a) yeruppu + '-ni' or '-ti' = yerrani or yerrati pusthakam (The book which is red)

b) pasupupachcha + '-ni' or '-ti' = pasupupachchani bandhi (The vehicle which is yellow)

c) a yerrani pusthakamu thiiskoandi

lit: that book which is in red color take

t: Take the book which is red color

Here in the above example, you are pointing out to a bunch of books and you are asking the other person to take the book which is red in color.

2f) Demonstrative Adjective:

Earlier we have discussed about the demonstrative pronouns, there you would find two pronouns ('i' (this - adjective), 'a' (that - adjective) which refers to an adjective. Since we have already discussed more about this topic, I will not discuss it again. If you have any doubts please refer to the sub heading "Difference between 'i' (this - adjective), 'a' (that - adjective), 'ye' (which? - adjective) and 'idhi' (this - noun) 'adhi' (that - noun) 'yedhi' (which? - noun)" in Lesson 4: Pronoun.

More Examples on Sentences with Adjective:

a) idhi okka andhamaina prapancham

lit/t: This is a beautiful world

b) adhi okka paatha illu

lit/t: That is an old place

c) koncham coffee ivvandi

lit: some coffee please give me

t: Please give me some coffee

d) adhi okka dhattamaina adavi.

lit/t: That is a thick forest

e) idhi ghataina vantakamu

lit/t: This is spicy food

f) avi subhramina niiLLu

lit/t: that is a clean water

g) athanu okka balaheenamaina abbaayi

lit/t: He is a weak boy

h) akkada chaala kukkalu unnaayi

lit/t: There are lots of dogs there

i) naaku aidhuguru snehithulu unnaaru

t: I have five friends

Exercises:

A) Choose the correct adjective as per the English translation.

E.g. aame okka _____ ammaayi (She is a short girl)

a. pottaina   b. podavaina   c. yethaina

Right Answer: pottina

1. athanu okka _____ abbaayi (He is a Tall boy)

a. podavaina   b. pottaina   c. vedalpaina

2. adhi okka _____ daari (That is a wide path)

a. podavina   b. pottina   c. vedalpina

3. nimma pandhu _____ pandhu (Lemon is a sour fruit)

a. pullanaina   b. tiyyanaina   c. ghataina

4. adhi chaala _____ naga (That is a very expensive jewel)

a. chinnadaina   b. khariidaina   c. vedalpaina

5. idhi _____ prashnaa? (Is this a difficult question?)

a. khashtamaina   b. viluvaina   c. chinna

6. akkada _____ iLLu unnaayi (There are lots of house's here)

a. chaalaa   b. viluvina   c. pottina

7. adhi okka _____ kukka (That is a fast dog)

a. veegamaina   b. pedhdhadaina   c. chinna

8. adhi _____ gadhi (That is a dark room)

a. chiikati   b. pedhdha   c. chinna

9. adhi okka _____ kukka (That is a white dog)

a. thellati   b. nallati   c. yerrati

10. adhi okka _____ kukka (That is a slow dog)

a. nidaanamaina   b. peddadina   c. chinna

B) Translate the following using the appropriate Adjectives.

Example: She is a beautiful girl (Polite)

Solution: aame okka andhamaina ammaayi

1) He is a thin boy.   _____

2) It is a red phone.   _____

3) Take the phone which is red.   _____

4) This is a tasty fruit.   _____

5) This is a heavy bag.   _____

6) That is a soft skin.   _____

7) It is a wet floor.   _____

8) I have seven brothers.   _____

9) It is a circular jewellery   _____

10) It is an ordinary coffee.   _____

Adjectives made from Verb Using the Suffix:

A verb can also be made as an adjective in past tense by adding the suffix '-nna' to the root of the verb. For making the verb as an adjective in the present and future tense you should add the suffix '-ne' to the root of the verb. These are called as Verbal adjectives.

Past Tense Adjective: Verb root + '-nna'

Present and Future Tense Adjective: Verb root + '-ne'

Examples:

1) Verb root 'thinu' (To eat))

a) Verb root: 'thinu' (To eat) + Adjective suffix for past tense '-nna' = 'thinna' (The one who ate)

b) Verb root: 'thinu' (To eat) + Adjective suffix for present tense '-ne' = 'thine' (The one who eats)

c) Verb root: 'thinu' (To eat) + Adjective suffix for future tense '-ne' = 'thine' (The one who will eat)

Now we will use these Verbal adjectives in a sentence.

- thinna ammaayi (The girl who ate)
- thine ammaayi (The girl who eats)
- thine ammaayi (The girl who will eat)

Now, we will use the Verbal adjective of the verb 'thinu' (to eat) in a sentence.

2) ninna thinna ammaayi maala vochchindhi

lit: yesterday, the girl who ate maala came

t: Maala, the girl who ate came yesterday.

3) I roju thine ammaayi maala vosthundhi

lit: today the girl who eats maala is coming

t: Maala, the girl who eats is coming today.

4) repu thine ammaayi maala vosthundhi

lit: tomorrow the girl who will eat maala will come

t: Maala, the girl who will eat will come tomorrow.

5) naatyam aade abbaaayi (Future verbal adjective)

lit/t: Dancing boy

In Detail: aadu (to play) (verb root) + '-ne' = 'aade'

6) paade ammaayi (Present verbal adjective)

lit/t: Singing girl

7) maatlaadina abbaayi (Past verbal adjective)

lit: who spoke boy

t: The boy who spoke

Important Note: Similar to English, using verb as an adjective (Verbal Adjective) is rarely used in Telugu. So, I haven't created any exercises for them. The Explanation and examples given above are just for your information so that when you come across such sentences with Verbal Adjective you shouldn't be surprised and you will know how to use them.

Adverbs:

An adverb is a word that describes or changes a verb, an adjective, clauses, sentences or another adverb. Adverbs in Telugu are used more extensively than in English. A noun can be made as an adverb by adding the suffix '-gaa'.

Examples: Similar to the examples you saw in the Adjectives, in order to change a noun into adverb just add the suffix '-gaa'.

Taste:

Noun	Telugu	Adverb Suffix	Adverb	English
Taste	ruchi	+ '-gaa'	ruchigaa	Tasty
Bitter	cheedhu	+ '-gaa'	cheedhugaa	Bitter
Sour	pulla	+ '-gaa'	pullagaa	Sour
Hot	kaaram	+ '-gaa'	kaaramgaa	Hot
Sweet	thiipi	+ '-gaa'	thiyyagaa	Sweet

For Example:

a) nenu guruvu gaa unnaanu.

lit: I teacher am

t: I am a teacher

Detail: 'guruvu' (Teacher) + '-gaa' = 'guruvugaa' (Adverb) (being a teacher)

nenu (I) – This is a Pronoun (another form of noun).

'guruvu' (Teacher) - This is also a noun, which says something about the other pronoun 'nenu', this noun tells us that the other noun is a teacher.

'unnaanu' (am) – This is conjugated verb of 'undhi'.

As you saw in the above, this sentence satisfies the entire rule that I have mentioned earlier, it contains a conjugated verb and two nouns, in which the one says that the other is a teacher. Hence, we change the noun which says about the other noun into an Adverb.

Thus, 'guruvu' (Teacher) (Noun) became guruvu gaa (teacher) (Adverb).

b) nuvvu andhamgaa unnaavu

lit: you beauty are

t: You are beauty (To be more precise: You are being beauty)

Detail: 'andham' (beauty) + '-gaa' (Adverb suffix) = 'andhamgaa' (being beauty) (Adverb)

c) athanu santhosham gaa thintunnaadu

lit: he happily is eating

t: He is eating happily

d) aavida haayigaa nidrapoyindhi

lit: she peacefully slept

t: He slept peacefully

e) mii bandi chaalaa shubram gaa undhi

lit: your vehicle very clean is

t: Your vehicle is very clean.

Important Note: Adverbs in Telugu are used much broader than in English. In Telugu, Adverbs are used for directions, manners etc. It will be complicated to study everything; as you will hardly use them. The rules and examples I have given above are frequently used, so it is essential that you understand and use them while forming sentence.

Exercise:

C) Choose the correct Adverb as per the English translation.

E.g. aavida _____ matlaaduthunnaaru (She is speaking beautifully)

a. andhamgaa   b. ashyamgaa   c. chinnagaa

Right Answer: andhamgaa

1. aayana _____ unnaadu (He is Tall)

a. pottigaa   b. podavugaa   c. chinnagaa

2. i pandhu _____ undhi (This fruit is bitter)

a. cheedhu   b. cheedhugaa   c. cheedhaina

3. I aahaaram _____ undhi (This food is sweet)

a. thiyyagaa   b. thiyya   c. thiipi

4. a kukka _____ undhi (That dog is white color)

a. thellagaa   b. thelupu   c. yhellanaina

5. ikkada iLLu _____ unnaayi (There were less house here)

a. thelupu   b. thakkuvagaa   c. thakkuvaina

D) Translate the following using the appropriate Adverb.

1) That boy was thin.   _____

2) I can run very fast.   _____

3) I could not eat fast.   _____

4) This fruit is very tasty.   _____

5) This bag is heavy.   _____

6) That skin was very soft.   _____

7) That floor was wet.   _____

8) I can sing very beautifully.   _____

9) That jewellery is circular.   _____

10) This coffee is ordinary.   _____

Solutions

Exercise A

1) a, 2) c, 3) a, 4) b, 5) a, 6) a, 7) a, 8) a, 9) a, 10) a.

Exercise B

1) athanu sannati/sannani abbaayi 2) adhi yerrati phone 3) yerrati phone thiisko 4) adhi ruchaina pandhu 5) adhi baruvaina sanchi 6) adhi mruduvaina charmam 7) adhi thadi nela 8) naaku yeduguru tammuLLu 9) adhi gundrati naga 10) adhi maamulu coffee

Exercise C

1) b, 2) b, 3) a, 4) a, 5) b.

Exercise D

1) a abbaayi sannagaa unnaadu 2) nenu veegam gaa parigethagalanu 3) nenu veegam gaa thinalenu 4) i pandhu thiyya gaa undhi 5) i bag baruvu gaa undhi 6) a charam chaalaa soft gaa / mrudhuvugaa undhi 7) a nela thadigaa undhi 8) nenu chaalaa andhamgaa padagalanu 9) a naga gundramgaa undhi 10) I coffee mamulgaa undhi

LESSON 2A: VOCABULARIES

Vocabularies

Kindly find the table below with useful Telugu vocabularies that are being used in this book. I would recommend you to memorize these vocabularies in your free time either by using the memrise app or by using the traditional method of reading and memorizing from the book. But don't spend too much time on it, some 15 minutes everyday day will be good.

The advantage of memorizing the vocabularies and reading the book at the same are many.

1) You will be able to recollect the vocabularies while reading the book.

2) You will be able to make multiple sentences apart from the examples I have given you because you have lots of vocabularies in your arsenal right now

3) Much easier to do the exercise from the book.

4) Helps you to practice pronunciation and many more.

	Telugu	English
1	pusthakam	Book
2	cheppu	To Say, Tell
3	ivvu	To Give
4	raayi	To Write
5	gaaru	Mr
6	nenu	I
7	nuvvu	You

	Telugu	English
8	miiru	You (Polite)
9	athanu/vaadu	He
10	aayana	He (Polite)
11	aame	She
12	aavida	She (Polite)
13	manamu	We (Listener Included)
14	meemu	We (Listener Not Included)
15	vaallu	They (Polite)
16	avi	Those
17	ivi	These
18	adhi	That
19	idhi	This
20	naa	My
21	nii	Your
22	mii	Your (Polite)
23	mana	Our (Listener Included)
24	maa	Our (Listener Not Included)
25	vaLLa	Their (Polite)

	Telugu	English
26	yenti	What?
27	yendhuku	Why?
28	yevaru	Who?
29	yekkada	Where?
30	yeppudu	When?
31	yeedhi	Which (Noun)?
32	ye	Which (Adjective)?
33	yela?	How?
34	yenni?	How Many?
35	yentha?	How Much?
36	I	This
37	a	That
38	ikkada	Here
39	akkada	There
40	ippudu	This Time, Now
41	appudu	That Time, Then
42	intha	This Much
43	antha	That Much

	Telugu	English
44	inni	This Many
45	anni	That Many
46	ila	Like This
47	ala	Like That
48	I roju	This Day or Today
49	a roju	That Day
50	ye roju	Which Day
51	indhuku	For This
52	andhuku	For That
53	itu vaipu	This Side
54	atu vaipu	That Side
55	i vaipu	This Side
56	a vaipu	That Side
57	ye vaipu	Which side?
58	thala	Head
59	kukka	Dog
61	abbaayi	Boy
62	ammaayi	Girl

	Telugu	English
63	illu	Home
64	vaahanam, bandhi	Vehicle
65	ninna	Yesterday
67	repu	Tomorrow
68	bhojanam	Food, Breakfast, lunch or dinner
69	shabdham	Sound
70	undeedhi	It Was
71	undhi	It Is
72	untundhi	It Will Be
73	unnaayi	Those Were
74	untaayi	Those Are
75	undeevi	Those Will Be
76	okka	A, One
77	shoplo	In the Shop
78	shopki	To the Shop
79	eruppu	Red
80	yeluka	Rat
81	pilli	Cat

	Telugu	English
82	pillulu	Cats
83	podhdhuna	Morning
84	madhyanam	Afternoon
85	raathri	Night
86	godugu	Umbrella
87	uppu	Salt
88	kuuragaayalu	Vegetables
89	manchi	Good
90	andi	Please
91	dhayacheesi	Please (Extreme)
92	viidhi	Street
93	varusa	Line
94	nela	Month
95	tharagathi	Class Room
98	gantalu	Hour, O'clock
99	nimishaalu	Minutes
100	banthi	Ball
101	kosam	For

	Telugu	**English**
102	kavaali	Want
104	akka	Elder Sister
105	thammudu	Younger Brother
106	amma	Mom
107	nunchi	From
108	valana	Because Of
109	varsham	Rain
110	kante	Than, That (Comparison)
111	batti	According To
112	paatashalaku	To the School
113	pani	Work
114	bhaarya	Wife
115	bhartha	Husband
116	thalupu	Door
117	koncham	Little
118	balla	Table
119	kindha	Under
120	chettu	Tree

	Telugu	English
121	suryudu	Sun
122	mabbulu	Clouds
123	cheruvu	Lake
124	puulu	Flowers
125	kitiki	Window
126	samayaniki	On Time
127	pedhdha varsham	Huge Rain / Lots of Rain
128	mancham	Bed cot
129	sahayam	Help
130	vodhdhu / odhdhu	Do Not Want, Do Not Need
131	paalu	Milk
132	kaadhu	No
133	avunu	Yes
134	avunaa?	Is That So? / Honestly?
135	kudhuruthundhi	Possible
136	kudharadhu	Not possible
137	kudharaledhu	Was not possible
138	ishtam	Like

	Telugu	English
139	ishtam undadhu	Do Not Like
140	ishtam ledhu	Did Not Like
141	thelusu	Know
142	theliyadhu	Do Not Know
143	ardham	Meaning
144	ardham ayindhi	Understood
145	ardham kaadhu	Do Not Understand
146	ardham kaaledhu	Did Not Understand
148	ledhu	There Is Not
149	chaalu	Enough
150	saripothundhi	Sufficient
151	saripodhu	Not Enough, Not Sufficient
152	akuudadhu	Should Not, Shall Not
153	prashna	Question
154	samadhaanam	Answer
155	aata	Game, Play
156	kuuda	Also
157	koduku	Son

	Telugu	English
158	kuthutru	Daughter
159	kavaalaa?	Do You Want?
160	ledha	Or Else, Otherwise
161	kaani	But
162	bhagha ledhu	Not Good
163	bhagha undhi	Is Good
164	andhukani	So, Because Of That
165	endhukante	Because
166	akali ga	Feeling Hungry, Hunger
167	tharuvatha	After That
168	cheppu	Slipper
169	pelli	Marriage
170	andharam/anni	All
171	inka	Still, Yet
172	inka ledhu	Not Yet
173	ayindhaa?	Is It Over?
174	untu	To Be / Have
175	cheyyi	To Do

	Telugu	English
176	saadhinchu	To Achieve
177	thirugu	To Wander
178	kuurcho	To Sit
179	le	To Raise / Get Up
180	vochcha	To Come
181	veLLu	To Go
182	bratuku	To Survive
183	padu	To Fall
184	avvu	To Become
185	aaduko	To Play
186	poyyi	To Pour
187	raayi	To Write
188	parigeththu	To Run
189	nadupu	To Drive
190	vesko	To Wear
191	kattu	To Build, To Tie
192	aruvu	To Scream
193	kadugu	To Wash

	Telugu	English
194	thuduvu	To Wipe
195	uthuku	To Wash Clothes
196	thiisei	To Remove
197	dhuvvu	To Comb
198	nettu	To Push
199	kottu	To Hit
200	vethuku	To Search
201	nammu	To Believe
202	doraku	To Get
203	vaadu	To Use
204	paadu	To Sing
205	matlaadu	To Speak
207	muyyi	To Close
208	konu	To Buy
209	ammu	To Sell
210	ventapadu	To Chase
211	piluvu	To Call
212	thinu	To Eat

	Telugu	**English**
213	kaalchu	To Shoot
214	cheppu	To Tell
215	thadumu	To Touch
216	vodhilai	To Leave
217	nilabadu	To Stand
218	chuudu	To See
219	chupinchu	To Show
220	pettu	To Keep
221	chadhuvu	To Read
222	nerchuko	To Learn
223	nerpinchu	To Teach
224	natinchu	To Act
225	thiisko	To Take
226	thiiskura	To Bring Along
227	thiiskuveLLu	To Take Away
228	pattuko	To Hold
229	maduvu	To Fold
230	thaagu	To Drink

	Telugu	English
231	vondu	To Cook
232	laagu	To Pull
233	gamaninchu	To Observe
234	navvu	To Laugh
235	naduvu	To Walk
236	marchipo	To Forget
237	theruvu	To Open
238	yeghuru	To Fly
239	chachipo	To Die
240	kalupu	To Mix
241	aloochinchu	To Think
242	ivvu	To Give
243	pampu	To Send
244	yekku	To Climb
245	adugu	To Ask
246	nimpu	To Fill
247	perugu	To Grow
248	yeeduvu	To Cry
250	cherupu	Erase
251	chimpu	Tear
252	thokku	Step On
255	kuttu	Stich
256	ki	To

	Telugu	English
257	lo	In
258	lopala	Inside
259	bayata	Outside
260	gurinchi	About
261	varaku	Till
262	lekunda	Without
263	dhaghghara	Near, At (For Location)
264	miidha	On
265	tharuvatha	After, Next
266	mundhu	Before
267	paina	Up
268	kindha	Down
269	aduguna	Bottom
271	poyina	Last/Previous
273	ku	At (For Time)
274	pakkana	Beside
275	madhyalo	In the Middle Of
276	dwaara	Through

LESSON 2B: BASIC TELUGU SENTENCES & ROLE PLAY SCENARIOS

Telugu Sentences:

Kindly find tables with useful Telugu sentences below and role play scenarios after that.

Note: It is advisable for the learners not to concentrate in learning sentences or role play scenarios before learning other lessons in this book because Telugu grammar is a bit different from English grammar. If you look at the Telugu sentences before learning Telugu grammar, you will get confused and find it difficult to comprehend the Telugu sentences. Whereas, when you learn Telugu grammar and then look at these sentences, then you will be able to understand and learn the sentences well.

The above statement is just a suggestion, as this is the best way to learn Telugu in my opinion. But there are some exceptions as well.

1. You could also learn these Telugu sentences and role play scenarios simultaneously along with other lessons (Telugu grammar), this would help you to understand Telugu grammar better and at the same time your Telugu vocabularies will improve.

2. Some of you might just want to learn few sentences in Telugu language to practice it with native Telugu speakers and you might not be interested in Telugu grammar at all. These tables and role play scenarios are for you.

The sentences in the below table will be provided as below form.

Example:

How are you doing?

tl: nuvvu yela chesththunnavu

lit: you how are doing.

In Detail: nuvvu - you, yela - how, chesththunnavu - doing (present tense).

Transliteration (tl) - This is the transliteration of the Telugu script, in simple words, this is how a Telugu pronunciation would be if it's written in Telugu.

Literally (lit) - Since the word order for many sentences are different compared to English, I have provided the literal translation of the Telugu script.

	English	Telugu	Literal Translation
1	Good morning	shubhoodhayam	good morning
2	Thank you	dhanyavaadhaalu	thank you
3	You are welcome	paravaleedhandi	it's okay
4	To learn	nerchuko	to learn
5	Very quickly	thondharaga	very quickly
6	Good	baagundhi	being good
7	To go	veLLu	to go
8	He goes	athanu veLthaadu	he goes
9	It is good	adhi baagundhi	it is good
10	What	yenti	what
11	Water	niillu	water
12	To drink	thaagu, thaagadaaniki	to drink
13	You want	miiku kavaali	for you want
14	Do you want?	miiku kavaalaa?	for you want?
15	What do you want?	miiku yem kavaali?	for you what want?
16	What do you want to drink?	miiku yem thaagaalani undhi?	for you what drink desire is there?
17	To eat	thinu	to eat
18	What do you want to eat?	miiku yem thinaalani undhi?	for you what eat desire is there?
19	To do	cheyyi	to do
20	What do you want to do?	miiku yem cheyyaalani undhi?	for you what do desire is there?
21	To come	ra, vochcha	to come
22	Do you want to come?	miiku raavaalani undhaa?	for you come desire is there?

	English	Telugu	Literal Translation
23	With me	naa tho	with me
24	Do you want to come with me?	miiku naa tho raavaalani undhaa?	for you with me come desire is there?
25	Today	I roju	this day
26	Do you want to come with me today?	I roju miiku naa tho raavaalani undhaa?	this day for you with me come desire is there?
27	Evening	saayanthram, saayankaalam	evening
28	This evening	i sayanthram, i sayankaalam	this evening
29	This night, tonight	I roju raathri	this night, tonight
30	Do you want to come with me this evening?	i sayanthram miiku naa tho raavaalani undhaa?	this evening for you with me come desire is there?
31	Will you come with me tonight?	i raathri nuvvu naa tho vasthaavaa?	tonight you with me will come?
32	When	yeppudu	when
33	When do you want to be here?	miiku yeppudu ikkada undaali?	for you when here be there?
34	Is it possible for you?	miiku kudhuruthundhaa?	for you is it possible?
35	Is it possible for you to come with me?	miiku naa tho raavadam kudhuruthundhaa?	for you with me for coming is it possible?
36	Will you come with me?	miiru naa tho vasthaaraa?	you with me will come?
37	Come with me	naa tho raa	with me come
38	To see	chuudu	to see
39	Bye	veLi vasthaanu	will go and come back
40	When do you want to see?	miiku yeppudu chuudaalani undhi?	for you when see desire is there?

	English	Telugu	Literal Translation
41	Can you see it? (lit: are you able to see it)	miiru adhi chuudagalaraa?	you that can you see?
42	Can you see it? (lit: are you able to view it)	miiku adhi kanapaduthundhaa?	for you that able to see?
43	I can	naaku kudhuruthundhi	for me possible
44	I want	naaku kavaali	for me want
45	When do you want?	miiku yeppudu kavaali?	for you when want?
46	If you want	miiku kavaali ante	for you want if
47	We want	maaku/manaku kavaali	for us want
48	You are coming	miiru vasthunnaaru	you are coming
49	We are coming	meemu/manamu vasthunnaamu	we are coming
50	Are you coming?	miiru vasthunnaaraa?	are you coming?
51	When are you coming?	miiru yeppudu vasthunnaaru?	you when coming?
52	I am coming	nenu vasthunnaanu	i am coming
53	Soon	ventene	soon
54	I'm coming soon	nenu ventene vasthunnaanu	me soon coming
55	To stay	undhu	to stay, to be / have
56	We are staying	meemu untunnaamu	we are staying
57	We are staying here	meemu ikkada untunnaamu	we are staying here.
58	We are staying here today.	meemu I roju ikkada untunnaamu	we are today here staying.
59	We are staying here this tonight	meemu i raathri ikkada untunnaamu	we tonight here staying
60	You are staying	miiru untunnaaru	you are staying
61	Are you staying?	miiru untunnaaraa?	are you staying?

	English	Telugu	Literal Translation
62	How	yela	how
63	We are going	memu veLthunnaamu	we are going
64	You are going	miiru veLthunnaaru	you are going
65	Are you going?	miiru veLthunnaaraa?	are you going?
66	I am going	nenu veLthunnaanu	i am going
67	Not	ledhu	not
68	Now	ippudu	now
69	Not now	ippudu kaadhu	now not
70	I want to see it	naaku adhi chuudaali	for me that see
71	But	kaani	but
72	I want to see it but not now	nenu adhi chuudaali kaani ippudu kadhu	for me that see but now not
73	Are you able to see it?	miiru chuudagalaraa?	are you able to see it?
74	I am able to see it	nenu chuudagalanu	i am able to see it
75	I am unable to see it	nenu chuudalenu	i am unable to see it
76	I am unable to see you	nenu ninnu chuudalenu	i you unable to see
77	I cannot see it	naaku adhi chuudadam kudharaledhu	for me that see cannot
78	I cannot see you	naaku ninnu chuudadam kudharaledhu	for me you see cannot
79	To stand	nilabadu	to stand
80	We understand	maaku ardham ayindhi	for us meaning came
81	Good / well	manchidhi	good / well
82	Very good	chaala manchidhi	very good

	English	Telugu	Literal Translation
83	We understand you	miiru cheppeedhi naaku ardham ayindhi	you saying for me meaning came. (lit: we are able to understand what you are saying")
84	More	chaala / yekkuva	more
85	It is very good	adhi chaala baagundhi	that very good
86	We don't understand	maaku ardham kaaledhu	for us meaning came
87	We don't understand it	maaku adhi ardham kaaledhu	for us that meaning came
88	We don't understand you	maaku miiru cheppeedhi ardham kaaledhu	for us you saying meaning came
89	Do you understand?	miiku ardham ayindhaa?	for you meaning came?
90	Do you understand it?	miiku adhi ardham ayindhaa?	for you that meaning came?
91	Do you understand me?	miiku nenu cheppeedhi ardham ayindhaa?	for you i saying meaning came?
92	Don't you understand me?	miiku nenu cheppeedhi ardham kaaledhaa?	for you i saying meaning doesn't come?
93	I'm sorry.	kshaminchandi	i'm sorry.
94	I'm sorry but ...	kshaminchandi kaani	i'm sorry but ...
95	I'm sorry but I cannot understand you	kshaminchadi kaani miiru cheppeedhi naaku ardham kaaledhu	i'm sorry but you saying for me meaning not coming
96	We are not staying long (time)	meemu yekkuva samayam undamu	we more time not staying
97	We cannot stay here long	meemu ikkada yekkuva samayam undadam kudharadhu	we here more time staying not possible
98	How long	yentha samayam	how time
99	To search	vethaku	to search

	English	Telugu	Literal Translation
100	We have	undhi	
101	How long can you stay here?	miiru yentha samayam undadam kudhuruthundhi?	you how time staying possible?
102	I'm sorry but I cannot search it	kshaminchandi kaani nenu adhi vethakalenu	i'm sorry but i that cannot search
103	I know	naaku thelusu	for me know
104	I know it	adhi naaku thelusu	that for me know
105	I don't know it	naaku adhi theliyadhu	for me that don't know
106	Where	yekkada?	where
107	I don't know where it is	adhi yekkada undho naaku theliyadhu	that where is there for me don't know
108	I cannot find it	naaku adhi vethakadam kudharadhu	for me that finding cannot
109	I could not find it	naaku adhi vethakadam kudharaledhu	for me that finding couldn't
110	I'm sorry, but I don't know where it is. I couldn't find it	kshaminchandi, kaani adhi yekkada undho nakku theliyadhu. naaku adhi vethakadam kudharaledhu	I'm sorry, but that where is there for me don't know. for me that finding couldn't
111	I understood	naaku ardham ayindhi	for me meaning came
112	I understood it very well	naaku adhi baagha ardham ayindhi	for me that very well meaning came
113	I don't understand you very well	miiru cheppeedhi naaku baagha ardham kaaledhu	you saying for me good meaning didn't come
114	To bring	thiisukuraa	(lit: pick it up and being)
115	Will you bring it to me?	naa dhaggaraki thiisuku vasthaaraa?	near me will you take and come?
116	We have it	mana dhaggara adhi undhi	us nearby that is there

	English	Telugu	Literal Translation
117	We don't have it	mana dhaggara adhi ledhu	us nearby that is not there
118	Do you have?	mii dhaggara undhaa?	you nearby is here?
119	Do you have it?	mii dhaggara adhi undhaa?	you nearby that is there?
120	Why	yendhuku	why
121	For me	naaku, naa kosam	for me
122	For you	miiku, mii kosam	for you
123	It is for me	adhi naaku	that for me
124	Why don't you understand me?	miiku nenu cheppeedhi yendhuku ardham kaadhu?	for you i saying why meaning not coming?
125	Something	yeedho, yedhainaa	Something
126	Can you bring me something now?	ippudu naaku yedhainaa thiisuku raagalaraa?	now for me something can you take and bring?
127	I must have it	naaku adhi undaaali	for me that must have
128	I cannot bring it to you now	nenu adhi mii dhaggaraki thiisuku raalenu	i that nearby you take and bring cannot
129	What do you have for me?	mii dhaggara naa kosam yem undhi	you nearby for me what is there
130	What can you bring me?	miiru naa kosam yem thiisuku raagalaru?	you for me what take and being along?
131	With you	mii tho	with you
132	I cannot bring it to you today, because I don't have it	nenu adhi mii dhaggaraki I roju thiisuku raavadam kudharadhu, endhukante adhi naa dhaggara ledhu	i that you nearby today take and brining cannot, because that me nearby not there
133	I couldn't bring it to you today, because I don't have it	nenu adhi mii dhaggaraki I roju thiisuku raavadam kudharaledhu, endhukante adhi naa dhaggara ledhu	i that you nearby today take and brining couldn't, because that me nearby not there

	English	Telugu	Literal Translation
134	You have to come with me	miiru naa tho raavaali	you with me must come
135	To give	ivvu	to give
136	We are giving	meemu isthnnaamu	we are giving
137	You are giving	miiru isthunnaaru	you are giving
138	I am giving	nenu isthunnaanu	i am giving
139	I am giving it to you	nenu adhi miiku isthunnaanu	i that for you giving
140	But I cannot give it to you today, because I don't have it.	kaani adhi miiku i roju ivvadam kudharadhu, endukante adhi naa dhaggara ledhu	but that for you today giving cannot, because that my nearby is not there
141	When do you want to have it?	miiku adhi yeppudu kavaali?	for you that when want?
142	Also	kuuda	also
143	Me too	nenu kuuda	i also
144	I don't smoke	nenu poga thaaganu	i don't smoke
145	need	avasaram	need
146	I need it	naaku adhi avasaram	for me that need
147	I don't need it	naaku adhi avasaram ledhu	for me that need is not there
148	I don't need it now	naaku adhi ippudu avasarm ledhu	for me that now need is not there
149	Do you need it?	miiku adhi avasaramaa?	for you that need?
150	When do you need it?	miiku adhi yeppudu avasaram?	for you that when need?
151	When do you want it?	miiku adhi yeppudu kavaali?	for you that when want?
152	I can bring it to you today.	nenu adhi miiku I roju thiisku raagalanu	i that for you today take and bring can

	English	Telugu	Literal Translation
153	I will bring it to you.	nenu adhi miiku I roju thiisku vasthaanu	i that for you today will take and bring
154	When can you bring it to me?	miiru adhi naaku yeppudu thiisku raagalaru?	you that for me when take and bring can?
155	When will you bring it to me?	miiru adhi naaku yeppudu thiisku vasthaaru?	you that for me when will take and bring?
156	When can you bring it to me? because I need it today.	miiru adhi nakku yeppudu thiisku raagalaru? endhukante naaku adhi kavaali	you that for me when take and bring can? because for me that want
157	When do you want it? I want it today, because I need it	miiku adhi yeppudu kavaali? naaku adhi I roju kavaali, endukante adhi naaku avasaram	for you that when want? for me that today want, because that for me need
158	At what time?	yenni gantalaku?	at what time?
159	At what time do you want it?	miiku adhi yenni gantalaku kavaali?	for you that at what time want?
160	At what time can you be here tonight?	miiru I roju raathri yenni gantalaku ikkada undagalaru?	you tonight at what time here can be here?
161	At what time do you want to be here?	miiru I roju raathri yenni gantalaku ikkada undaali?	you tonight at what time here want to be here?
162	At what time can you be here today?	miiru I roju yenni gantalaku undagalaru?	you today at what time can be there?
163	At what time will you be here?	miiru yenni gantalaku ikkada untaaru?	you at what time here be there?
164	To arrive, to come	vachcha	to arrive, to come
165	At what time will you arrive tomorrow?	miiru repu ikkada ki yenni gantalaku vasthaaru?	you tomorrow here at what time will come?
166	At what time can you be here tomorrow?	miiru repu ikkadaki yenni gantalaku raagalaru?	you tomorrow here at what time can come?
167	How long can you stay here today?	miiru yentha samayam I roju ikkada undagalaru?	you how much time today here can stay?

	English	Telugu	Literal Translation
168	How long will you stay here?	miiru ikkada yentha samayam untaaru?	you here how much time will be there?
169	To wait	undu	to wait
170	Will you please do it for me?	miiru adhi naa kosam chesthaaraa?	you that for me will do?
171	When will you do it for me?	miiru adhi naa kosam yeppudu chesthaaru?	you that for me when will do?
172	Will you stay here with me?	miiru naa tho untaaraa?	you with me stay?
173	To say / to tell	cheppu	
174	Will you tell me?	miiru chepthaaraa?	will you tell me?
175	When will you tell me?	miiru naaku yeppudu chepthaaru?	you to me when will tell?
176	Will you tell me where it is, because I could not find it	miiru adhi yekkada undho chepthaaraa,endhukante adhi vethakadam naaku kudaraledhu	you that where is there will tell, because that finding for me couldn't
177	I don't know	naaku theliyadhu	for me don't know
178	I'm sorry, but I don't know where it is. I could not find it	nannu khaminchandi, adhi yekkada undho naaku theliyadhu. adhi vethakadam naaku kudaradhu	me sorry, that where is there for me don't know. that finding for me couldn't
179	We go, we are going	meemu veLthaamu, meemu veLthunnaamu	we go, we are going
180	We will go	meemu veLthaamu	we will go
181	We didn't go	meemu veLLaaledhu	we didn't go
182	Where are you going?	miiru yekkadiki veLthunnaaru?	you to where going?
183	Where do you want to go?	miiru yekkadiki veLLaali?	you to where go desire?

	English	Telugu	Literal Translation
184	Is there	undhi	is there
185	I want to go there, but I cannot go there today	naaku akkadiki veLLaali ani undhi, kaani naaku I roju veLLadam kudaradhu	for me to there go desire is there, but for me today going cannot
186	Busy	pani lo unnanu	i am at work
187	Business / store	vyaapaaram/ kottu	business / store
188	I am busy	nenu pani lo unnaanu	i am at work / working
189	I am very busy today	naaku ippudu pani undhi	for me now
190	I will be busy	nenu pani lo untaanu	i at work will be there
191	How long are we staying?	manamu entha samayam untunnaamu?	we how much time staying?
192	How long can we stay here today?	manamu entha samayam I roju ikkada undagalamu?	we how much time today here can stay?
193	How long will we stay here today?	manamu entha samayam I roju ikkada untaamu?	we how much time today here will stay?
194	How long do you want to stay here?	miiru ikkada entha samayam undaali?	you here how much time want to stay?
195	How long are you staying here?	miiru ikkada entha samayam untunnaaru?	you here how much time staying?
196	How long are you staying?	miiru entha samayam untunnaaru?	you how much time staying?
197	Do you stay here?	miiru ikkada untaaraa?	you here staying?
198	Are you staying here?	miiru ikkada untaaraa?	you here staying?
199	Come!	randi/vachcha	Come!
200	Bring it!	adhi thiiskurandi	that take and come
201	Bring it to me today!	adhi I roju naa dhaggara ki thiiskurandi	that today near me take and come

	English	Telugu	Literal Translation
202	Are you bringing it to me today?	miiru I roju naa dhagaariki thiiskuvasthaara?	you today near me take and come?
203	Do you bring it to me?	miiru naaku adhi thiiskuvasthaaraa?	you for me that take and bring
204	Bring it to me!	naaku adhi thiiskuvasthaara?	for me that take and bring?
205	We are waiting	meemu yedhuru chusthunnamu	we are waiting
206	We didn't wait	meemu yedhuru chudaledhu	we didn't wait
207	We will not wait	meemu yedhuru chudanu	we will not wait
208	Why are you waiting?	miiru enduku yedhuru chusthunnaaru?	you for what waiting?
209	Why do you wait?	miiru enduku yedhuru chusathaaru?	you for what wait?
210	Wait, please!	undandi	wait, please!
211	Will you please wait for me here tomorrow?	miiru naa kosam repu yedhuru chusthaaraa?	you for me tomorrow will wait?
212	Wait for me!	naa kosam yedhuru chudandi	wait for me!
213	Are you waiting for me?	miiru naa kosam yedhuru chusthunnaraa?	you for me wait?
214	Will you please wait for me	miiru naa kosam yedhuru chusthaaraa?	you for me will wait?
215	Can you wait for me?	miiru naa kosam chudagalaraa?	you for me can wait?
216	Where will you wait for me?	miiru naa kosam yekkada yedhuru chusthaaraa?	you for me where wait?
217	They are staying	vaaLLu untunnaaru	they are staying
218	How long do we stay here?	manamu entha samayam ikkada untaamu	we how much time here stay
219	I am staying	nenu untunnaanu	i am staying

	English	Telugu	Literal Translation
220	I am not staying here	nenu ikkada undadam ledhu	i here staying not
221	I am coming with you	nenu mii tho vasthunnaanu	i with you coming
222	Wait!	undu	wait!
223	Will you (please) wait	undandi	will you (please) wait
224	Will you wait?	miiru yedhuru chuusthaaraa?	you will wait?
225	I will wait for you	nenu nii kosam yedhuru chusthaanu	i for you will wait
226	I'm not going to stay here	nenu ikkada undadam ledhu	i here staying not
227	To buy	konu	to buy
228	I'm going to buy it	nenu konadaaniki veLthunnaanu	i for buying going
229	I will buy it	nenu adhi kontaanu	i that will buy
230	We won't buy it	meemu konamu	we wont buy it
231	Expensive	vela yekkuva	price high
232	It is very expensive	idhi vela yekkuva	this price is high
233	We are going to buy it because we want to have it	meemu adhi konadaaniki veLthunnaamu, endhukante maaku adhi kavaali	we that for buying going, because for us that want
234	He will buy it	athanu adhi kontaadu	he that will buy
235	He will be here soon	athanu thondharagaa ikkada untaadu	he soon here will be there
236	She will be here soon	aame thondharagaa ikkada untundhi	she soon here will be there
237	Ready	thayaaru	ready
238	It is ready	adhi thayaaru ga undhi	that being ready is there
239	Already	mundhe	already

	English	Telugu	Literal Translation
240	He is here already	athanu ikkada mundhe unnaadu	he here already is there
241	I have it already	adhi mundhe naa daggara undhi	that already near me is there
242	Beautiful	andhamina/ andham ga	being beautiful
243	It is very beautiful	adhi chaala andham ga undhi / adhi chaala andaminadhi	that very being beautiful is
244	She is very beautiful	aame chaalaa andham ga undhi	she very being beautiful is
245	It is ready already	adhi mundhe tayaaru ayindhi	that already ready became
246	Everything	anni/antha	everything
247	Everything is ready already	antha thayaaru ga undhi	everything being ready is there
248	He is staying	athanu untunnaadu	he is staying
249	She is staying	aame untundhi	she is staying
250	It is staying	adhi untundhi	it is staying
251	All of them	andharu	all of them
252	They are all staying here	vaaLLu andharu ikkada untaaru	they all here stay
253	All of them are staying here	vaaLLu andharu ikkada untunnaaru	they all here staying
254	My friend	naa snehithudu (male) / naa snehithuraalu (female)	my friend
255	My friend is not staying	naa snehithuraalu undadam ledhu	my friend is not staying
256	My friends are not staying here	naa snehithuraalu ikkada undadam ledhu	my friends here staying not
257	We are all staying here	meemu andharam ikkada untunnaamu	we all here staying

	English	Telugu	Literal Translation
258	He is coming soon	athanu ventane vasthunnaadu	he soon coming
259	He is bringing it to me	athanu adhi naa dhaggaraki thiiskuvasthunnadu	he that near me take and come
260	He will bring it to you tomorrow	athanu adhi nii dhaggaraku repu thiiskuvasthaadu	he that near you tomorrow take and come
261	When are you going to bring it to me?	nuvvu adhi naa dhaggaaraku eppudu thiiskuvasthaavu?	you that near me when take and come?
262	Will you please bring it to me	adhi miiru naa dhaggaaraku thiiskuvasthaarandi	that you near me take and come please
263	Will you bring it to me tomorrow	adhi miiru naa dhaggaraku repu thiiskuvasthaaraa?	that you near me tomorrow will take and come
264	I want it	naaku adhi kavaali	i that want
265	To know	naaku thelusu	for me know
266	We know	maaku thelusu	for us know
267	You know	miiku thelusu	for you know
268	Do you know?	miiku thelusaa?	for you know?
269	He knows	athaniki thelusu	for he know
270	They know	vaaLLaki thelusu	for them know
271	Can you tell me?	miiru naaku cheppagalaraa?	you for me can tell?
272	Will you tell me where it is ...... because I cannot find it	miiru adhi yekkada undho naaku cheppagalaraa?...... endhukante adhi naaku kanapadaledhu	you that where is there to me will say? ...... because that for me couldn't find
273	At home	intlo	at home
274	I am going home	nenu intiki veLthunnanu	i to home going
275	I will stay home	nenu intlo untaanu	i at home will stay

LESSON 2C: ROLE PLAY SCENARIOS

Telugu Role play scenarios:

Kindly find below role play scenarios at the end of this book.

Note: It is advisable for the learners not to concentrate in learning sentences or role play scenarios before learning other lessons in this book because Telugu grammar is a bit different from English grammar. If you look at the Telugu sentences before learning Telugu grammar, you will get confused and find it difficult to comprehend the Telugu sentences. Whereas, when you learn Telugu grammar and then look at these sentences, then you will be able to understand and learn the sentences well.

The above statement is just a suggestion, as this is the best way to learn Telugu in my opinion. But there are some exceptions as well.

1. You could also learn these Telugu sentences and role play scenarios simultaneously along with other lessons (Telugu grammar), this would help you to understand Telugu grammar better and at the same time your Telugu vocabularies will improve.

2. Some of you might just want to learn few sentences in Telugu language to practice it with native Telugu speakers and you might not be interested in Telugu grammar at all. These tables and role play scenarios are for you.

The sentences in the below scenarios will be provided as below form.

Example:

How are you doing?

tl: nuvvu yela chesththunnavu

In Detail: nuvvu - you, yela - how, chesththunnavu - doing (present tense).

Transliteration (tl) - This is the transliteration of the Telugu script, in simple words, this is how a Telugu pronunciation would be if it's written in Telugu.

Scenario 1: Restaurant

Let's look at a scenario between friends who wants to eat biriyani in a restaurant:

Person A & B are friends and Person C is a waiter in the Restaurant they go to.

A: shall we go and eat in a restaurant today?

tl: manamu restaurant ki veLLi tindhaamaa?

B: sure, we can go, but to which restaurant?

tl: thappakunda veldhaam. kaani ye restaurant?

A: We shall go to Paradise restaurant.

tl: manamu paradise restaurant ki veLdhaamu

In Restaurant:

C: Welcome Sir.

tl: lopaliki randi

C: Have you reserved a table?

tl: table reserve chesaaraa?

B: Yes.

tl: chesaanu sir

C: Under which name?

tl: ye peru thodi?

B: Mr. Vincent

A: The restaurant is totally full today.

tl: I roju restaurant nindu ga undhi.

B: Yes, there are many people.

tl: avunu, chaala manchi unnaaru andi

C: What would you like to eat?

tl: meeru yem thinaali anukuntunnaaru?

B: 2 plate Biriyani, please.

tl: rendu plates biriyani teeskurandi

C: Would you like something to drink?

tl: meeru yeminaa thaagaali anukuntunnaaraa?

B: One orange juice and one coffee.

tl: okka orange juice okka coffee

C: do you want anything else?

tl: meeku inka yemina kavaalaa?

B: One moment, please.

tl: okka nimisham andi

C: What do you want to eat, Sir?

tl: meeru yem thintaaru sir?

B: one plate chilli chicken.

tl: okka plate chilli chicken

C: Anything else?

tl: inka yemina kavaalaa?

B: No, that's all for the moment.

tl: ledhu, pppatiki inthe

C: okay

B: Please hurry.

tl: thondaragaa

C: okay

Situation: After sometime, the waiter provides the food and the two friends enjoy their meal and after they are done eating, the waiter comes back and….

C: How was the meal, do you want anything else?

tl: bhojanam yela undhi? meeku inka yemina kavaalaa?

B: the meal was delicious; no, we don't want anything else.

tl: bhojanam chaalaa bagundhi. ledhu, maaku inkem vodhdhu

A: Please give us the bill

tl: bill ivvandi

C: Here you go, Sir.

tl: idhigondi sir

A: (pays the bill with a small tip)

C: Thank you very much.

Scenario 2: Post office

Let's look at a scenario between a person and a shop keeper:

Person A is the one who wants to send the post and Person B is the shop keeper.

A: Where is the post office?

tl: post office yekkada undhi?

B: The post office is on the left.

tl: post office yedama pakka undhi

A: At what time does the post office open?

tl: post office yenni gantalaku therusthaaru?

B: The post office opens at 10.00 a.m.

tl: post office podhdhuna 10 gantalaku therusthaaru

A: At what time does the post office close?

tl: post office yenni gantalaku muusthaaru?

B: The post office closes at 5 p.m.

tl: post office aidhu gantalaku muusthaaru

A: I want to send this letter by post.

tl: nenu okka letter pampaali

A: What is the postage for a letter to Delhi, India?

tl: delhi ki postage yentha?

B: It is 50 Rupees.

tl: yaabhai rupaayalu

A: In how many days will it reach to Delhi?

tl: adhi delhi ki yeppudu cheruthundhi

B: It will reach in 3 days.

tl: muudu rojullo cheruthundhi

A: Where must I put the letter?

tl: letter yekkada pettaali

B: Put it in the mail box.

tl: mail box lo veyyandi

A: Please give me postage stamps.

tl: postage stamps ivvandi

B: Here you go, 50 Rupees please

tl: idhigondi. yaabhai rupaayalu

A: Where is the head office?

tl: Head office yekkada undhi

B: It is behind the post office.

tl: Post office venaka undhi

A: I need 2 postcards as well please.

tl: naaku rendu post cards kuuda kavaali

B: Here you go.

tl: idhigondi

Scenario 3: Shopping for clothes

Let's look at a scenario between 2 people in a clothes shop:

Person A is the one who wants to buy clothes and Person C is the clothes seller.

C: Good morning ma'am, what do you want?

tl: good morning andi yem kavaali?

A: Good morning. I want to buy a shirt.

tl: good morning andi. naaku shirt kavaali

C: What color do you want?

tl: yem color kavaali?

A: I prefer blue.

tl: naaku blue color shirt kavaali

C: Light blue or dark blue?

tl: light blue naa dark blue naa?

A: Show me both.

tl: rendu chupinchandi

C: Here you go. But what size do you want?

tl: idhigondi. kaani, miiku ye size kavaali?

A: A large shirt.

tl: large shirt kavaali

C: A cotton or silk shirt?

tl: cotton aa, silk aa?

A: A cotton shirt. My husband doesn't like wearing silk shirts.

tl: cotton shirt, maa husband ki silk shirt ishtam ledhu

C: Here you go, Anything else ma'am?

tl: idhigondi. inka yemina kavaalaa?

A: Yes, I also want a saree.

tl: avunu. naaku saree kuuda kavaali

C: The sarees are on the first floor.

tl: sarees, first floor lo unnaayi

A: I want to buy this tie.

tl: naaku okka tie kavaali

C: Sure ma'am.

tl: thappakundaa madam

A: How much is it?

tl: idhi yentha?

C: It costs 500 Rupees.

tl: aidhu vandhalu

A: Oh, but this is too expensive for me. I want to see another tie.

tl: oh avuna. vela chaalaa yekkuva undhi. naaku inkoka tie chupinchandi

C: Do you like this tie?

tl: i tie chustharaa?

A: Yes, this one is better, how much is it?

tl: ah, idhi bagundhi. yentha?

C: Only 200 Rupees.

tl: rendu vandhalu mathrame

A: Okay, I will buy this one.

tl: sare. nenu idhi thiiskuntaanu

A: where should I pay for the shirt and the tie?

tl: nenu i shirt ki tie yekkada pay cheyyaali?

C: At the cash counter over there.

tl: cash counter lo pay cheyyandi

A: Thank you.

Scenario 4: Shopping for fruits

Let's look at a scenario between 2 people in a fruits shop:

Person A is the one who wants to buy clothes and Person C is the fruits seller.

A: How much does the apples cost?

tl: apples yentha

C: The apples cost 300 Rupees per kg?

tl: Kg muudu vandhalu

A: That's very expensive.

tl: chaalaa yekkuva undhi

C: The prices are fixed ma'am.

tl: fixed price mam

A: Give me half a kilo of apples.

tl: naaku arakilo apples ivvandi

C: Anything else?

tl: inka yemina kavaalaa?

A: How much are the grapes?

tl: Grapes yenthaa?

C: 150 Rupees a kg.

tl: nuuta yaabhai rupaayalu

A: Are they fresh?

tl: fresh ga unnaayaa?

C: Yes ma'am.

tl: avunandi

A: Okay, then give me 2 kgs of grapes.

tl: sare naaku rendu kilolu grapes

C: Is that all?

tl: anthenaa

A: Yes, how much is that in total?

tl: motham yentha ayindhi

C: 450 Rupees. Will you be paying by cash or credit card?

tl: naalugu vandhala yaabhai rupaayalu. Card aa, cash aa?

A: Do you accept debit cards?

tl: miiru debit card thiiskuntaaraa

C: Yes ma'am.

A: Ah, that's good. Here you go.

tl: sare. idhigondi

Scenario 5: Airport, Immigration control section

Let's look at a scenario between 2 people in Airport, Immigration control section:

Person A is a Tourist and Person B is an Immigration control officer.

B: How long will you stay here? What is the purpose of your visit?

tl: miiru ikkada yenni rojulu untaaru? yendhuku vochchaaru

A: I am here for holidays.

tl: nenu holidays ki vochchaanu

B: Your passport please.

tl: mii passport ivvandi

A: Here it is.

tl: idhigondi

B: Do you have anything else to declare?

tl: miiru inka yemina declare cheyyaalaa?

A: Yes, a small bottle of perfume and TV.

tl: ah, okka TV, bottle of perfume

B: Do you have any luggage?

tl: inka yemina luggage undhaa

A: Yes, a big bag.

tl: ah, okka pedhdha bag undhi

B: Please show me your Flight ticket and Visa.

tl: mii flight ticket visa chupinchandi

A: Here they are.

tl: idhigondi

B: You will have to pay custom duty for the TV, please fill this form and pay the money at the counter.

tl: miiru TV ki custom duty pay cheyyaali. form nimpandi

A: Okay, Thank you

Scenario 6: Railway station

Let's look at a scenario between 2 people at the Railway station:

Person A is a Tourist and Person B is an office at the railway ticket counter.

A: What time does the train to Hyderabad leave?

tl: hyderabad train yenni gantalaku veLthundhi

B: At 10:15 AM.

tl: padhimpav

A: And what time does it arrive?

tl: yenni gantalaku vosthundhi

B: At 2:30 PM.

tl: raathri rendunara

A: Is it a direct train?

tl: direct train aa?

B: Yes, it's a direct train.

tl: avunu

A: The train leaves from which platform?

tl: train ye platform lo undhi

B: It leaves from platform 2.

tl: rendava platform

A: A ticket for Hyderabad, please.

tl: hyderabad ki okka ticket

B: One-way or return?

tl: one way aa., return kuuda naa

A: One-way.

B: First class or second class?

tl: first class aa, second class aa

A: First class.

B: Do you want a window seat?

tl: miiku window seat kavaalaa?

A: Yes, I want the window seat.

tl: avunu

B: Here, your seat number is 11.

tl: mii seat number 11

A: Thank you very much, Sir.

B: Here is your ticket and your reservation, 300 Rupees.

tl: idhigondi mii ticket. muudu vandhalu

A: Thank you.

tl: thanks andi.

Scenario 7: Doctors clinic

Let's look at a scenario between a doctor and a patient:

Doctor: How are you?

tl: yela unnaaru

Patient: I have a headache.

tl: naaku thala noppi gaa undhi

Doctor: Do you feel tired as well?

tl: miiku tired ga undhaa

Patient: No, but I am unable to sleep well.

tl: ledhu kaani nidhra raavadam ledhu

Doctor: Okay, I will give you some medicine for you to sleep well and something for your headache as well.

tl: miiku nenu nidhra ki thalanoppiki tablets isthaanu

Patient: Doctor, I am also having some eye pain.

tl: Doctor, naa kannu kuuda noppi ga undhi

Doctor: Please lie down, I will check your eyes.

tl: padukondi nenu chusthaanu

Doctor: Your eyes seems to be fine, maybe its because of your headache.

tl: mii kannu bagane undhi. May be thala noppi valana kaavachu

Doctor: Please take the medicine that I gave you and if you still have problem with your eyes please come and meet me again.

tl: nenu ichina medicine veskondi. inka problem unte maLLi randi

Patient: Thank you doctor. How much is the doctor fee?

tl: thanks andi. mii fee yentha?

Doctor: 500 Rupees and here is the prescription.

tl: aidu vandhalu, prescription thiiskoandi

Scenario 8: Asking for directions

Let's look at a scenario between 2 people asking for directions:

Person A is a Tourist and Person B is a stranger he meets on the road.

A: Excuse me, please.

tl: excuse me

B: Yes?

tl: cheppandi

A: How do I get to the Castilla Hotel?

tl: castilla hotel ki yela veLLaali?

B: Go straight ahead. Then take the second street on the right. That is the Solomen Street.

tl: straight ga velli right ki vellandi. adhi solomen street

A: The second on the right?

tl: second right aa?

B: Yes, exactly. Then take the first street on the right. The Castilla Hotel will be on the left.

tl: avunu. tharuvatha first right thiiskoandi. akkada castilla hotel undhi

A: Thank you very much. Goodbye!

tl: thanks andi

Scenario 9: Random conversations

The below are random conversations:

9. Random Conversation

A: What is your profession?

miiru yem chesthaaru

B: I am a doctor.

nenu doctor ni

A: What does your father do?

mii nanna garu yem chesthaaru

B: My father is a dentist.

maa nanna garu dentist

A: What does your mother do?

mii amma garu yem chesthaaru?

B: My mother is a housewife.

maa amma housewife

10. Random Conversation

A: I just bought a necklace.

nenu ippude okka neckless konnanu

B: Made of gold or silver.

Gold aa silver aa

A: I bought a diamond necklace

nenu dimond neckless konnaanu

B: Where did you bought this necklace?

miiru i neckless yekkada konnaaru

A: I bought it in the Ganesh jewelers

nenu ganesh jewelers lo konnaanu

B: It looks very beautiful; shall we go to the jewelry shop together this weekend?

idhi chaalaa andha gaa undhi. manamu i weekend a shop ki kalasi veldhaamaa

A: Yeah definitely.

ah thappakundaa

11. Random Conversation

A: I want to go shopping. Where is the market?

nenu shopping ki veLLaali. market yekkada undhi

B: What do you want to buy?

miiru yem konaali

A: I want to buy clothes and fruits.

nenu battalu, pandhlu konaali

B: To buy clothes, you can go to the Ganesh market and to buy fruits, go to the fruit market.

battalu ganesh market lo konachu. pandlu fruit market lo konachu

A: Thank you very much.

thanks andi

www.ingramcontent.com/pod-product-compliance
Lightning Source LLC
Chambersburg PA
CBHW080002130626
46550CB00013B/2627